Saul Bellow's Heart

Saul Bellow's Heart

A Son's Memoir

Greg Bellow

BLOOMSBURY

New York   London   New Delhi   Sydney

Published by Bloomsbury USA, New York

All papers used by Bloomsbury USA are natural, recyclable products made
from wood grown in well-managed forests. The manufacturing processes
conform to the environmental regulations of the country of origin.

LIBRARY OF CONGRESS CATALOGING-IN-PUBLICATION DATA

Bellow, Greg.
Saul Bellow's heart : a son's memoir / Greg Bellow. — 1st U.S. ed.
p. cm.
ISBN 978-1-60819-995-2
1. Bellow, Saul.   2. Novelists, American—20th century—
Biography.   3. Fathers and sons—Biography.   I. Title.
PS3503.E4488Z849 2013
813'.52—dc23
[B]
2012035407

First U.S. Edition 2013

1 3 5 7 9 10 8 6 4 2

Typeset by Westchester Book Group
Printed and bound in the U.S.A. by Thomson-Shore, Inc., Dexter, Michigan

To my mother, Anita Goshkin Bellow Busacca,
whose message to me and to all was "Go for it!"

To my father, Saul Gordon Bellow, whose message was
"If you go for it, make sure it's worthy of the family name."

And to my wife, JoAnn Henikoff Bellow,
whose faith in me never wavers.

CONTENTS

"Old Saul": The Literary Patriarch

AWAKENED BY A GRAVE
ROBBERY

ON A VISIT to Chicago when I was eight, I witnessed a terrible argument, in Yiddish, between my father and grandfather. Driving away from his father's house, Saul started to cry so bitterly he had to pull off the road. After a few minutes, he excused his lapse of self-control by saying, "It's okay for grownups to cry." I knew his heart was breaking. I knew because of the bond between my father's tender heart and mine.

As Saul's firstborn, I believed our relationship to be sacrosanct until his funeral, an event filled with tributes to his literary accomplishments and anecdotes about his personal influence on those in attendance that set in motion my reconsideration of that long-held but unexamined belief. As we drove away, I asked my brother Dan how many sons he thought were in attendance. His answer, literally correct, was three. I disagreed, feeling that almost everyone there considered him- or herself to be one of Saul's children. That first glimpse of the extent of Saul Bellow's patriarchal influence awakened me to the impact of a literary persona I had assiduously avoided while he was alive.

I grew up in a household filled with books and lively conversation, bound together by a commitment to seeking and telling the truth. I came to share the value my parents placed on culture, which included the quiet solitude that my father thought essential to writing. His study door was firmly closed every morning, a sign of the barrier Saul drew between writing and living. For decades I ferociously protected his privacy, literary and personal, which both of us connected with those hours of his writing day. As a child I learned not to disturb him. As an adult I turned a blind eye to the literary persona and to the public furor over his fame, which reached an apex in Stockholm. After 1976 I boycotted all events held in his honor. Saul became offended, but I felt the limelight contaminated the private bond I was trying to protect.

The posthumous tributes to the author who altered American literature came as no surprise. Hoping that my son Andrew, who took no interest in Saul's literary career, would learn a bit about a grandfather who had paid him scant attention, I urged him to watch the discussion of Saul that aired soon after his death on the PBS *NewsHour*. The next day Andrew said, "What was all the fuss about Grandpa changing American literature? He was just a grouchy old man." Andrew's response succinctly captured a distinction between the private man and the literary lion that was just beginning to dawn on me.

As soon as Saul died, his lawyer, Walter Pozen, set the tone for what was to come. Instead of calling the family, Walter phoned the public media. I learned of my father's death on my car radio. The chosen speakers at Saul's funeral were Martin Amis, the literary "son," and Ruth Wisse, the dutiful Jewish "daughter." Though no family members were asked to speak, I rose to praise Saul's widow, Janis, for her devotion during my father's last years. Strangely silent was another literary heir, Philip

Roth, who, like a kind of brooding Hamlet, wandered the edges of the funeral in deep thought. Soon thereafter, the *New Yorker* published a series of rambling letters Saul had written to Philip about the origins of his novels, which I thought underlined the uniqueness of the deep literary connection between them. I was transfixed as I read these letters because the mental confusion apparent in Saul's repetitive accounts was like a stream-of-consciousness narrative that filled blank after blank in stories my father had told me.

To keep my grief private, I avoided the flood of obituaries until urged to read Leon Wieseltier's tribute in the *New Republic*. I was not surprised that he looked up to my father as an intellect or found him a man of great charm and wit. But his tribute was so complete a conflation of the famous author and my father, the man, that I could barely recognize Saul. As well, Mr. Wieseltier seemed to have found the basis of a deep rapport with my father that touched on personal affections I considered my birthright. In the following weeks I heard and read many anecdotes and accounts that claimed a similar special closeness with Saul Bellow the literary patriarch. I took them to be distinctly filial and soon came to feel that dozens of self-appointed sons and daughters were jostling in public for a position at the head of a parade that celebrated my father's life. By now irked by the shoving match at the front of the line, I asked myself, "What is it with all these filial narratives? After all, he was *my* father! Did they all have such lousy fathers that they needed to co-opt mine?"

Before his death I had purposely placed the private man I did not want to share into the foreground. Infuriating as they were, the filial narratives and flood of posthumous tributes awakened me to the powerful effect of my father's novels, to his status as a cultural hero, and to my lack of appreciation of the public side of him that I had been trying to avoid.

As I grieved and as the distinctions between the private man and the public hero were filtering though my consciousness, someone suggested I might find solace in reading Philip Roth's *Patrimony*. I was deeply struck by a scene in which the elder Roth catches his son taking notes, no doubt in preparation for writing about moments that Philip's father considered too private to expose. I asked myself, "Has Philip no shame?" But Roth's decision to write about his father's last days forced me to think about what to do with the father who resides within me—a man whose deepest desire was to keep his thoughts and his feelings strictly to himself.

Among the myriad ways Saul protected his privacy was an almost complete refusal to reflect aloud upon his inner life. He abetted this lack of transparency by giving ambiguous answers to personal questions or by offering parabolic stories with meanings that could be extracted by a perceptive listener or reader. As he and I walked down Boston's Commonwealth Avenue in 1990, out of the blue my father said: "Your old pal Oscar Tarcov thought Ben Turpin was a very funny man. In a brief film sketch about moving into a new apartment, Turpin carried furniture up several flights and carefully arranged it. Turpin's redecorating concluded when he threw a couch through the living room window, shattering the glass. Asked why he did not open the window first, he answered, 'I'm an artist. I can't be bothered.' That's the way it was for your mother and me." After fifty years of decoding his stories, I knew Saul was telling me about the cultural attitudes and unconventional behavior that held my parents' marriage and our young family together.

At a Bellow family dinner several weeks after Saul's death, an argument broke out over the recently declared war in Iraq. My brother Adam maintained that our government's actions were correct and legitimate while I vehemently questioned the war's rationale and its ethics. Later, my cousin Lesha (Saul's niece, Grandma's namesake, and my senior by six years) commented that watching us disagree was like watching "young Saul" (me) argue with "old Saul" (Adam).

Our father was always easily angered, prone to argument, acutely sensitive, and palpably vulnerable to criticism. But I found the man Lesha called "young Saul" to be emotionally accessible, often soft, and possessed of the ability to laugh at the world's folly and at himself. Part of our bond was grounded in that softness, in humor, and in the set of egalitarian social values I adopted. Saul's accessibility and lightheartedness waned as he aged. His social views hardened, although he was, fundamentally, no less vulnerable. The earlier tolerance for opposing viewpoints all but disappeared, as did his ability to laugh at himself— much to my chagrin. His changes eroded much of our common ground and taxed our relationship so sorely that I often worried whether it would survive. But Lesha's comment highlighted the essential biographical fact: there could never have been an "old Saul," the famous author, without the "young Saul," the rebellious, irreverent, and ambitious man who raised me.

The impulse to write a memoir that gives equal weight to the lesser-known "young Saul," the father I love and miss, meant going against a lifetime of keeping a public silence to protect his privacy and our relationship. But I was also swayed by important external considerations. I wanted my children to learn about their grandfather. And I felt an obligation to open wide the eyes of my two younger brothers, who know only "old Saul" as a father. Several recent biographical articles of poor quality alerted me to the scholarly need for a portrait that reveals Saul's complex nature, one written by a loving son who also well knew his shortcomings. I have found Saul Bellow's readers, toward whom he felt a special love, intensely curious about the man whose fame rests partly on the complexity of his prose, partly on his desire for privacy, and partly on a lifetime of hiding behind parabolic stories, jokes, metaphors, and complex logical rationales when they suited his needs.

But what truly prompted me to write are the intense dreams that have taken over my nights. As my father's presence faded from my daily thoughts, I was often wakened from an anxious sleep, desperately trying to hold on to fleeting memories. I took my nocturnal anxiety as a warning from a recently deceased father to preserve what remains of him before it is lost—perhaps forever.

For decades my father told me stories about the past, mostly in private or in the company of family, often over late afternoon tea. Friends and family have added impressions and vignettes—charming and not so charming. I have eagerly listened to narratives accompanied by astute observations and politely endured others so wildly inaccurate as to be amusing. For every story I am told, I know ten, and by now my memory has become a repository of the complexity and the humanness of Saul Bellow, the man, the father, and the author who wrote from his head and his heart. Awakening as the dreamt stories threaten to slip away reveals my fear that those treasures will be lost if not put to paper.

Continuing to turn a Sammleresque blind eye to Saul Bellow's literary fame would also be to ignore lessons I learned right after my father's death: that writing was his raison d'être, so much so that I honored his life by rereading all the novels in temporal sequence as my way to sit shivah (to formally mourn); that all the posthumous filial narratives were more than the grave usurpation I considered them to be at first; that writing primarily from memory and about feeling suits me, a recently retired psychotherapist skilled in unraveling murky narratives. And perhaps most important, that my father looked most directly into the mirror when he wrote, providing, through his novels, a window into his frame of mind and a reflective self he took pains to protect in life.

In the novels I often find what amount to familiar snapshots from the Bellow family album, images of people, stories, and lives I know well. Thoughts and feelings my father places in the mouths of his narrators are, on occasion, so clear to me that, at moments, I feel as if I am peering over the shoulder of Saul Bellow the author as he writes in my father's diary. My rereading strengthens impressions I had garnered in our quiet conversations, and I take them as an invitation to move thoughtfully between the works of fiction and the life of a man who took such pains to protect what Saul called his "inner life." In *Dangling Man* the narrator, Joseph, describes a heart surrounded by a thicket "seldom disturbed" as his least penetrable part. I was raised by a man who surrounded his heart with a thicket that I was able to penetrate from time to time, though it remained difficult for both of us to fathom.

Despite my doubts about writing publicly, I have determined to learn more about my father, to reassess my patrimony as a writer's son, and to have my say. I can no longer climb into

Saul's lap as he sat at the typewriter, hit the keys, and leave my gibberish in his manuscripts as I did at three. Nor can I visit Saul in his dotage and stir up fading embers of our past. I can visit his gravestone and, in the Jewish tradition, put another pebble on it. But my "Pop" deserves more from his firstborn, as full and as honest a written portrait as I can render. Shutting my study door and struggling to find my voice on paper as I listen to Brahms or Mozart, as he did every day for more than seventy years, is as close as I can now get to my dead father.

"YOUNG SAUL":
THE REBELLIOUS SON

Chapter One

PARADISE: 1915–23

SHROUDED BY THE passage of more than a century and the thousands of miles between Lithuania and Chicago, my only palpable connections to my great-grandparents and the previous generations are a few photographs and what Saul called my "Litvak tongue," a propensity for sour-tasting food he cultivated by feeding me pickled herring when I was six months old. Everything I know about my Bellow side came to me through Saul's vivid accounts, told and retold.

My paternal grandfather, Abram Belo, whose name is Russian for the color white (as in Belarus), was born in Dvinsk in 1878 and grew up in Lithuania. Family lore has it that his father, Berel Belo, was a harsh parent. As a young man Abram's brother Willie joined a Bund, a left-wing organization linked to labor unions. Berel was having none of this transgression, and as a punishment he apprenticed Willie to a brush maker. Being consigned to a manual trade was a terrible humiliation for a Jewish boy from an aspiring family. Worse, the bristles came from pigs, animals Jews are forbidden to touch or to eat. Perhaps as much as anything else to escape their father, Willie and his two sisters, Hanna and Rosa, chose to leave Russia for Lachine, a poor suburb of Montreal, Canada.

Berel had Abram studying for a rabbinical career before his son was six. Not long thereafter, Abram began to live at the seminary, but poor physical conditions and the rabbis' brutality toward their students alienated my grandfather. He quit during his teens. From then on, skeptical about religious belief, Abram chose a worldly path, and by age twenty-four he was living illegally, beyond the Pale of Jewish Settlement (areas permitted under czarist law), in St. Petersburg. Although common among Jews at the turn of the century, living outside the Pale was dangerous. My grandfather was in a precarious situation and bribed the authorities to prevent exposure.

Abram worked at a company that imported Egyptian onions and Turkish figs, luxury items that he later claimed to have sold to the czar and wealthy residents of St. Petersburg. In a photograph my grandfather is sitting with a group of co-workers and looking dapper. The impression I garnered from my father is that Abram was a raconteur, a glib and entertaining fellow who was good to have around, though better at telling a story than at strenuous labor.

The Gordins, my grandmother Lescha's family, were also from Lithuania, a town named Dagda, near Riga. Moses Gordin, my great-grandfather, was a rabbinical scholar renowned for being able to recite lengthy sections of the Babylonian Talmud from memory. The one picture of him, secured without his knowledge because Orthodox Jews would not let themselves be photographed, shows a tiny man with a flowing beard and penetrating eyes. His appearance, which my father always thought otherworldly, made a deep impression on Saul, who thought his own eyes, facial structure, and capacious memory similar to his maternal grandfather's.

Moses Gordin had twelve children, but his family was sufficiently prosperous to support his religious studies without the need for him to engage in degrading physical labor. As adults, several of his children, including my grandmother Lescha, moved to St. Petersburg. Another brother went to South Africa and made a fortune before returning to live in St. Petersburg. Two or three Gordin brothers ran a restaurant that bore the family name, an indication of their proficiency in working the system despite the complexities of living where they were not legally permitted.

My grandmother first saw her prospective groom when a matchmaker brought Abram Belo to the Gordin house. Before being considered a worthy suitor, the young man had to be vetted by the Gordin male hierarchy by demonstrating his religious knowledge. As a former seminary student, Abram had no trouble impressing them as my grandmother, smitten by this handsome young man, looked on from behind a curtain. Both of my grandparents were well educated. Consistent with her romantic inclinations, Lescha enjoyed reading Pushkin.

Lescha Gordin was twenty-five and Abram Belo was twenty-seven when they married in 1905. The wedding was so grand that years later, in Lachine, when he and his family were in desperate financial straits, Abram's sisters often complained of what they considered its excess. At the time, however, the marriage proved to be a financial windfall for Abram, thanks to the Gordins' generous dowry. The newlyweds lived in a large house and had servants. In 1906, their first child, Zelda, was born; in 1908 their son Movscha arrived; and in 1911, Samuel.

The growing Belo family owned a country house to which

they escaped from St. Petersburg in summertime. Though Abram continued to import vegetables, his in-laws did not think he had a good head for business. They were dismayed when he quickly went through Lescha's substantial dowry and requested a second large sum. But the Gordin brothers, particularly the one who had made his fortune in South Africa, were generous toward their sister and her young family.

In 1912 the police cracked down on Grandpa. Abram was convicted of illegal residence and was nearly deported to Siberia before a Gordin brother arranged for the family to get out of the country. According to Saul, the papers that allowed them to leave Russia were "the best forgeries money could buy."

The entire family was on the same boat to Canada, but because they were traveling on forged papers the children were instructed not to acknowledge their father during the journey. The Belos landed at Halifax, Nova Scotia, where their westernization began. An immigration official changed Grandpa's name to Abraham Bellow, while Zelda and Movscha became Jane and Morris. Samuel and Lescha's names survived unscathed.

The family left the material comforts of Russia for a perilous life in the New World. My grandmother was permanently separated from her family. All of our relatives in Canada were on the Belo side of the family. Lescha never returned to Russia and dearly missed her family. When news of a brother's death from typhus arrived by post, she wept bitterly. By all accounts, my grandmother was often sad and morose. The strains imposed by poverty and an immigrant life weighed heavily upon her. Furthering her isolation, Lescha learned neither French nor English. In the New World she read sentimental novels in Yiddish that frequently brought her to tears.

By 1913, the Bellows were living in Lachine, the Montreal suburb where several Belo siblings had settled already. The factories and streets were filled with immigrant populations in a polycultural community my father captures in a 1992 autobiographical sketch, "Memoirs of a Bootlegger's Son." But inside the house the Bellow family preserved the old country along with its religious and cultural customs. Lescha kept a strictly kosher kitchen and insisted that her children study Hebrew, the Torah, and music. Yiddish was the family's primary language, and even in later years when discussing serious family business, Saul and his siblings would lapse into the familiar tongue of their childhood.

The struggling Bellow family rented a small house in a slum where rat droppings encrusted their front steps. Sam and Morrie shared a bed. In the 1990s several family members were granted brief access to the house, and my cousin Lesha told me later how tiny and dark the rooms were. Soon the Bellows moved into the same house as Rosa and Max Gameroff, Abraham's sister and brother-in-law. Rosa was a sharp-eyed businesswoman, and the Gameroff children, several years older than Morris and Sam, were hardworking boys. Uncle Max didn't share Rosa's ambition, but she had enough drive for two, and the couple began buying up property in town. Because Abraham was unable to make comparable success, frictions boiled over between a brother in need of money and a sister who not only refused to help him but twisted the knife when she said no. Kindhearted Uncle Max actually lent Abraham the capital to start a dry goods store after Rosa refused because she considered her brother's partner lazy and their location poor. Sure enough, the enterprise soon failed, fueling Rosa's doubts and sharpening her tongue. In addition to the dry goods store, Abraham began a series of failed enterprises that included the junk business and even a brief foray into matchmaking. Things were so bad that my grandfather considered farming, a vocation for which he was ill suited, but Lescha vetoed a rural life, which would have isolated her children from the schooling and cultural pursuits upon which she insisted.

Abraham could not make any economic progress in Lachine. A man full of ambitions and schemes to get rich, he was unwilling to work for someone else but unable to support his family as a businessman. My grandfather was always either unemployed or working fitfully. Saul's narrator Moses Herzog, in the novel that takes his last name for a title, describes his father as a man of sufficient charm to lure birds out of trees. Abraham possessed a similar charm, but his skill as a raconteur did not suit him in Montreal as it had in St. Petersburg. Out of work and often at home, his audience was now limited to his wife and children and his stories were told around the kitchen table.

The family's precarious financial situation was worsened by a schism between my grandparents when it came to spending their limited income. On one side was the struggling Abraham, egged on by Rosa Gameroff, a pragmatist bent on making money in the New World who wanted his children to earn their keep. On the other side was Lescha, who insisted her children be exposed to learning, culture, and scholarship, which Abraham considered expensive, time-consuming enterprises that took able hands away from the work that would ease his financial and physical burdens.

Abraham's failure to earn an adequate income aggravated his already volatile temper. He often blamed parenthood for his im-

poverishment and gave each of his boys a whack to cover their presumed sins when he got home from a day of hard work. Morrie, the oldest, largest, and most willful, silently took the brunt of his father's abuse. Abraham called him the Yiddish equivalent of "Tubby," which was meant to shame my uncle for his costly habit of eating too much. As adults, Saul and Sam charitably chalked up Abraham's anger to the frustrations of immigrant life, but Morrie rarely, if ever, talked about his father's beatings.

Into this family, Solomon Bellow was born on June 10, 1915. According to a story Saul told over and over, perhaps embellished and perhaps not, the doctor who delivered him was found in a tavern, intoxicated, by one of the Gameroff boys who was sent to fetch him when my grandmother went into labor. When Saul arrived, Jane was nine, Morrie seven, and Sam four. Th family living quarters were so cramped that he slept in a ' ambulator his first year. Morrie always claimed to be his ' er's favorite, but a nursing baby brother was a serious cor Lescha doted on her youngest, who was frail and of Saul's aunt Jenny, Uncle Willie's wife, who was chi' Saul's first years, also doted on him, singing him in English that she mangled with her Yiddish was deemed old enough to leave the peramb his brothers in a common bed, where M on his baby brother by pinching him and fingers. Yet, outside the house, Morr they were very close. Sam, while Saul, avoided as much of the fam'

Saul loved to tell the earthy claimed to remember. At thr ing a desire for Lescha's br

own shirt and exposed his useless nipple, a message that Saul was too old to nurse and that all he could expect from his father and the world was cold comfort. On another occasion, Sam was very sick and kept the household up all night with his coughing. Annoyed, his father said, "Let him die already." Yet Saul made it clear that somehow, despite his complaints and beatings, Abraham let his sons know he cared about them.

Saul emphasized the family's poverty and often told a story about asking his father to buy him an ice cream cone as they walked down the street in Lachine. My father gave two versions of Abraham's response. In the one he usually told, Grandpa opened his coin purse and showed Saul that it did not contain even the required penny. In the other, he hid the coin from Saul, who discovered it behind a fold. The first version touches on the extent to which the Bellow family lived on the edge, while the second hints at Abraham's resentment over the financial demands of four growing children. Saul attributed the absence of toys in the house to a lack of money, but there was a trunk full of fancy memorabilia and clothes left over from St. Petersburg that became playthings for the Bellow children. A ˙mbol of the opulence left behind in Russia, its contents be-˙ne Saul's repository of imaginative possibilities, and he co-˙ed the handle of a Russian samovar to use as a pistol.

˙ll the children studied Hebrew, but Morrie and Sam were ˙ groomed by Abraham to go into business. However, ˙ insisted that funds be set aside for music lessons for Jane, ˙riageable daughter, and for Saul, despite her husband's ˙ts about every penny she spent. She was frugal and ˙ enough money to send a bit to her brothers in Rus-˙d fallen on hard times after the Revolution of 1917.

Jane studied the piano and Saul took violin lessons. His teacher, as was the custom, administered physical punishment for poor performance. My father told me that he kicked the teacher in the shins, an unthinkable act of defiance for which he was severely punished by his father. Saul adopted his mother's cultural values, which descended from the Gordin family's roots in Talmudic scholarship. His facility for language and prodigious memory enabled him to quote long passages from Genesis in Hebrew at three or four years of age. Many years later, Abraham told my mother, "The family thought Saul was a genius until he was five."

Like many immigrant families with insufficient incomes, the Bellows took in boarders. One, a man simply called "the boarder" by the family, made a deep impression. Separated from his family in Russia, he spent time with the Bellow children in lieu of his own, and confided in Lescha. A lonely melancholic, he took to tippling and frequenting bordellos, drinking up his pay and dooming any possibility of sending for his wife and children. The boarder would come home in his cups, complaining about his boss or singing in Yiddish: "Ein, zwei, drei, vier, fünf, die vanzen dansen" (One, two, three, four, five, the bedbugs dance). Another of his songs, the meaning of which became apparent when I grew up, translates as: "Alone, alone, alone with my ten fingers alone."

In *Herzog*, as seen through the eyes of young Moses, the family's boarder returns home drunk, disheveled, and singing loudly enough to awaken the family and the neighborhood. At the urging of Mother Herzog, Father Herzog, who is wearing his fine St. Petersburg nightshirt, gets out of a warm bed to help the boarder up the stairs and out of his soiled clothes. His

wife's compassion is enough to stir even Father Herzog to sacrifice his own comfort for the benefit of another human being.
Even as a young boy, Saul could see the benign effects of his
mother's kindness and her ability to soften my grandfather's
harshness.

The extra money from the boarder's rent allowed the Bellows to buy my aunt Jane a piano after she showed a musical
aptitude so strong that she pretended to play an imaginary piano on the walls. By 1920 Jane was fourteen and a budding
young woman whose marital prospects took high priority. In
typical Jewish fashion, Jane was being groomed to marry a "professional" man. In order to cultivate the refinements that were
required to attract such a match, she was accorded privileges,
such as elegant clothes and a musical education, as soon as the
family could afford to pay for them. Abraham, initially scornful
of such luxuries, did not hesitate to show off Jane's musical accomplishments to impress guests in the Bellow home.

In his seventh year, Saul, suffering from a misdiagnosed case of
peritonitis, spent six months on the children's ward of a tuber-
culosis sanatorium. A surgical drain made out of a safety pin
was placed in his abdomen. The doctors held out little hope for
his recovery. Saul read his chart and understood the gravity of
his condition. Around him, little kids died in the night, leaving
no trace but an empty bed come morning.

Used to being doted on by his mother, Saul woke up every
morning eager for his family's company. Now, away from everyone familiar, he was lonely and bored. There was little to do on
the ward; reading the funny papers filled but a few minutes. A
woman volunteer who read the New Testament aloud to the

children served as one of the few distractions. She made a deep impression on Saul by exposing the lonely and frightened boy to Jesus. Saul secretly fell in love with Jesus as a man who loved mankind and suffered without complaint. Surrounded by other boys who taunted him for being Jewish, he quickly realized that loving Jesus was a complicated matter best kept to himself on the ward and from his parents. Though I never heard Saul make a connection between his love of Jesus and his indirect style of personal communication, I have often wondered whether Jesus's use of meaning-filled parables strengthened my father's inclination to communicate via stories.

The weekly visits to the children's ward were limited to a single adult family member, so Lescha and Abraham took turns riding the tram to see their son. Both cautioned Saul to behave, pressing him to control his temper when teased. On one occasion, Saul's siblings accompanied both parents to the hospital, even though they weren't allowed to see him. After the visit, Saul went to the window to look down on his family. He opened the window as they tried to throw a bag of forbidden candy to him. When they failed to get it to him, they left and ate it themselves. Saul told this story with humor that barely concealed his disdain for the readiness of self-interest to assert itself among the Bellows.

Living in the sanatorium required a different form of emotional toughness than enduring his father's beatings or teasing from the non-Jewish boys without complaint. Saul was, no doubt, bereft after visits that reminded him of life at home. But he put up a brave front and reserved his tears until after his parents left. In *Herzog*, Saul touches on the kind of toughness, the suppression of self-pity, he came to think was a requirement of day-to-day immigrant life. A young Moses Herzog is dragged into an alley and sexually assaulted. After the attack, the lad returns home and eats his soup, uttering nary a word. Later, as an adult, Moses observes that there was no room to be a frightened little boy and remarks that "the tender-minded must harden themselves."

Unhappy with Saul's absence and concerned by the slow pace of his recovery, Lescha took him out of the sanatorium to nurse him back to health sooner than the doctors thought safe. My father often described the journey back home, during which Lescha pulled him on a sled rather than making him walk. A similar scene is described in *Herzog* when Moses's mother drags him through the snow on a sled as they return from the hospital. Watching Mother Herzog struggle, an old woman warns her not to sacrifice her strength for the sake of her children. Moses, who well understands the old woman's warning, knows he is taking advantage of his mother but selfishly lets her continue to struggle. I must wonder if, when Lescha passed away ten years later, my father asked himself whether her life had been shortened by the family burdens she so willingly assumed.

After nearly a decade in Lachine, Abraham remained unable to support his family by legitimate means. He built a still on the outskirts of town and began selling a few illegal bottles of whiskey to locals. Many Jewish immigrants were making larger profits running rum into New York State during Prohibition, and Abraham soon acquired an ambitious partner who urged him to expand. But in order to make the whiskey salable in America, bootleg hooch had to pass for legitimate brands with recognized labels. Abraham had labels printed, and it became a family game to sit around the kitchen table gluing them onto bottles filled with the cheap stuff. It was great fun when he asked, "What shall we make this bottle, children, White Horse or Three Feathers?"

The life of a bootlegger was fraught with dangers for which my grandfather was ill prepared. Unlike the large operators, he could not afford to pay off the police, hire a truck, or form reliable New York connections. Spurred by ambition, the two small-time bootleggers tried to move a truckload over the border only to be double-crossed, most likely by the driver they recruited from a large operator unwilling to tolerate new competition. Hijacked and beaten, Abraham walked home bloodied, his bootlegging career over.

During the years the Bellows spent in Lachine, living on the edge drew the young family close. Everyone pulled his or her own weight, and individual needs were deferred for the common good. In the middle of winter, five-year-old Saul's chore was to go out into the backyard, break the ice that had formed over the brine, and retrieve several pickles for the family meal. As the kid brother, he took great pride in his contribution to the sense of shared responsibility that he later called "family feeling."

Despite the external chaos, privation, and even his father's beatings, Saul treasured the years in Lachine and looked back on them wistfully whenever life dealt him a blow. Uncle Willie's story offers a partial explanation. Having escaped from his fate as a brush maker in Russia, he worked in a fruit store in Lachine, where, with great aplomb, he would snap open paper bags for his customers before filling them. To my father, that confident gesture personified a type of order and optimism the New World offered immigrants.

The deep roots and the sense of belonging that my father felt within his family are revealed in *Dangling Man* when Joseph, as a child, takes it upon himself to shine all of the family's shoes. Blissfully happy in the service of those he loves, the boy feels such a sense of belonging that nothing can dislodge him from his chosen spot. As an adult, the duty, loyalty, and shared sacrifice that had afforded Saul a sense of safety became a sacred memory. My father returned to that "family feeling" in times of personal adversity, and it was so powerful in him that he expected it to extend into the next generation through his sons.

My father talked of Lachine as an Eden, a place without evil. In *Herzog*, a young Moses, touched by his father's palpable suffering after a flawed bootleg deal, creates a paradise by finding nobility in his father's failure. Though just a lad, Moses understands Papa Herzog's poor judgment and the threat to the family's survival it has caused. Rather than turning his back on his father, Moses calls Papa Herzog "my king," ennobling him as a man brought low by immigrant circumstance. A son not only turns a blind eye to his father's failure but also finds admiration rather than the pity or the blame that might crush them both.

Chapter Two

PARADISE LOST: 1924–37

FAILURE AS A bootlegger was the last straw, and Grandpa left Lachine for Chicago to work in his cousin Louie Dworkin's bakery. It was a comedown for a man of high ambition, but four hungry children allowed him no choice. Six months later, in the summer of 1924, Lescha and the Bellow children were smuggled across the U.S. border in the back of a bootlegger's truck. In Detroit they boarded a train for Chicago, where Cousin Louie and his wife, Rose, picked them up at Union Station in their convertible. Rose drove the Bellow family to their new home. She was the first woman Saul had ever seen behind the wheel, a sign of the heady air of freedom my father felt the moment he set foot in Chicago.

Before the family joined him, Abraham had shaved off the mustache he had worn for years, and his altered appearance initially frightened Saul. Exhausted by the hard physical labor of his night shift, Grandpa came home around breakfast time, his clothes white from flour. While he slept all day, Lescha had to keep the kids quiet to avoid angering him and provoking a beating.

Abraham and Lescha soon realized that the opportunities

afforded by life in America were superior to those in Canada. The children went off to school and excelled, and the Bellow family settled in. Abraham soon tired of working for someone else and keeping baker's hours. Lescha saved up enough money from his earnings for him to start a business delivering wood to bakeries. Soon he was selling coal, a form of fuel that was just coming into use to heat homes. Within five years, the Carroll Coal Company was providing a comfortable income and the earlier disagreements about working to help out the family versus getting an education faded into the background.

Anything was possible, especially in a wide-open city like Chicago. Street life flourished and the newspapers were filled with accounts of bloody rivalries between gangsters that fascinated the already bookish Saul. He told me that bodyguards toting tommy guns escorted Colonel Robert McCormick, the *Chicago Tribune*'s publisher, to his office on Michigan Avenue. My father captured the attraction of the underside of life in Chicago in the short story "Something to Remember Me By," where a gullible adolescent boy becomes victim to a nasty prank played by a bunch of his brother-in-law's streetwise pals.

The opportunities to make fast money in freewheeling Chicago appealed to Morrie. At fifteen, he was already working and turning over his earnings to Lescha, but soon he began to see angles and eventually to make political connections that Abraham could never imagine. As he became expert in the ways of capitalism, Morrie withdrew from the close-knit family and his rivalry with Saul took the form of deriding the high cultural interests his kid brother was developing.

Saul's continuing need for protection from his father and from the bullying of his older brothers required him to move beyond physical strength and master the mental toughness which was the common currency of Bellow men. My father did so by developing an intense interest in Harry Houdini and Teddy Roosevelt. Both famous men had strengthened their physiques and minds through disciplined training. Houdini, a Jew from a similar immigrant background, had mastered every muscle. Saul began to exercise regularly studied and tried to emulate Houdini's skills, practicing his tricks to Abraham's bewilderment.

Acting strong covered Saul's emotional weakness, which he associated with his mother and with women and which he found intolerable within himself. His solution to that vulnerability was to embrace rational argument, a strategy that allowed him to channel his massive intelligence, quick tongue, and volatile temper. Thus he was able to fend off his father and his brother's derision. According to Morrie's daughter, for years Morrie and Saul argued vehemently over the meaning of words, with one or the other running to the dictionary to settle matters. The competition between the brothers was so intense that in his Nobel lecture Saul cited a desire to exceed his brothers as a motivation to excel. And the rivalry never abated: just before his death (long after both Morrie and Sam were dead), Saul said to Sam's daughter Lesha, "I showed them."

Unlike Saul and Sam, Morrie hated to talk about the family's past, but I have little doubt that my father's portrait of Simon March, Augie's older brother in *The Adventures of Augie March*, sheds light on the origins of Morrie's cynicism. In this novel about life in America for first-generation Jews, Simon exemplifies how the hardness just under the veneer of the American dream can take its toll on an idealistic young man. In the book's early pages, Simon is the high school valedictorian and an Eagle Scout who fully embraces the myth that everything is possible if you subscribe to the nation's values and try hard. His romantic notions of happiness are shattered after he falls in love but is disqualified as a suitor because he has insufficient wealth and status to suit his beloved's family. Landing with a thud, Simon quickly absorbs the correct social lesson. Everything is possible in the good old U.S. of A. if you have the money.

Morrie suffered a similar romantic disappointment. The life lesson my uncle extracted was that warm sentiment, even of the kind exemplified by Lescha, was a sucker's game. Whatever softness he may have had was kept hidden from the world, though it likely fueled his propensity for throwing his financial success in everyone's face, particularly his baby brother's. For decades Morrie called Saul a sap for letting the opportunities and benefits available in America pass him by. Even as late as my childhood, a trip to Morrie's included a visit to his closet, from which my uncle would extract "old" suits and shirts and toss them on the bed. "You look like shit," he'd say to Saul. "Take these." And take them Saul did. Until I was a teenager, Saul's dress shirts were monogrammed with MGB, Morrie's initials.

Sam was successful at avoiding conflict with family, but he paid a high price. As a young man, Sam was accepted to medical school and was about to start when the family determined that he would go into the coal business. While my grandfather was the titular boss, Sam ran the business for decades and subtly kept his father in check. Lesha told me that he got up early and made sure to get to work before Grandpa because Sam did not trust his judgment. Under Sam's direction the business continued to prosper. I remember visits to the coal yard in the early 1950s with my grandfather and uncle camped out around a potbellied stove in a dreary, sooty wooden shack surrounded by a yard full of what looked like mountains of coal. Sam once said, likening himself to the mentally retarded brother in *Augie March*, "So I'm the dummy who stayed home."

Jane's special treatment continued in Chicago. She was given her own room and a fur coat, luxuries that irritated her brothers, since the always-contentious family assets were now lavished upon its marriageable daughter. Jane sacrificed a love match to marry my uncle Charlie, who had the one and only necessary qualification to be a son-in-law: a dental degree. Jane readily perpetuated Abraham and Lescha's aspirations, becoming a middle-class wife and mother who emphasized appearance at all cost.

By the time Saul entered Tuley High School in 1929, the Bellows had lived in Chicago for five years. The coal business was providing a comfortable income and the family had moved to the affluent side of Humboldt Park. The Bellow children grew older and everyone in the family, with the exception of Grandma Lescha, expanded their horizons. In the narrow world of Lachine, Lescha's old-world attitudes had held sway. But, as Saul's poignant story of their trolley rides illustrates, in Chicago she was out of her element. In the 1920s, you could identify pharmacies by the large mortar and pestle that hung above the street entrance. On rides home, Grandma, who never learned to read or write English, prepared to get off every time she spied a mortar and pestle because there was one near the Bellow house. Saul had to tell her each time that they were not home yet, and she would sit down, only to rise again at the sight of the next one.

In Saul's early teens, two contradictory forces exerted their pull. He was reading voraciously, spending his free time in libraries, and soaking up books and ideas like a sponge. At the same time, he was lured by street life. When it came to street smarts, Saul's friend Sam Freifeld had a huge head start on my father. Sam's politically connected father, Benjamin Freifeld, owned a pool hall where the boys spent their free time. Benjamin, who was confined to a wheelchair, was a man who somehow mixed complex notions about life with a passion for life that Saul found appealing. My father told me that Sam's father was the model for William Einhorn in *The Adventures of Augie March*, a man Augie describes as "superior," who takes the impressionable lad under a protective wing and teaches him valuable life lessons.

Einhorn is the prototype for a series of men Saul called "reality instructors" who filled his life and his novels, men who either understood or purported to understand how the world works. Augie March, a young man hungry to acquire worldly knowledge, moves from one person's scheme for living to the next. Throughout his life, my father also sought out advice when he could not understand or did not want to deal with what a writer's life threw at him. Yet, despite relationships that often lasted for years, most of the "reality instructors" and the ideas they put forward sooner or later failed to satisfy. But Saul's characterization of William Einhorn stands out because Einhorn cares deeply about Augie and offers the impressionable young man a model of thinking about living that goes beyond the abstract ideas from books that so disappointed in life application. Abraham also cared deeply about Saul, but an immigrant father could not offer him the lessons about life in America that his son desperately sought.

By 1932, the year of Saul's high school graduation, the Depression had tightened its grip on America. Radical political ideas became popular, particularly among Jewish immigrants who hadn't been free to express their opinions in the Old World. The optimism spawned by Karl Marx, the Russian Revolution, and, most of all, the idealism of Leon Trotsky took hold of Saul and his friends. Saul's commitment to left-wing ideas put him directly at odds with Abraham, who, despite experiencing the burdens of living under the czar, was dead-set against the communists. Bitter arguments, some over politics, erupted between father and son and continued to do so for decades.

The Humboldt Park neighborhood was on fire with a political consciousness that fueled left-leaning factions at Tuley High School. Saul attended rallies and debates, but he was never willing to commit wholeheartedly to any faction. Leon Trotsky's *A History of the Russian Revolution* had just been published in English and was on sale at Marshall Field's, a large department store in Chicago's Loop. The book's brisk sales caused concern for my father's friend Rudy Lapp and his, presumably Stalinist, faction. In keeping with the politically passionate character of the times and the bitter rivalry between the Trotskyites and the Stalinists about the merits of expanding the revolution beyond Russia, Rudy's comrades initiated a direct action by assigning him the mission of going downtown to steal the remaining copies, presumably to prevent them from falling into the "wrong" hands, which Rudy did with success.

In Humboldt Park and at Tuley High School, Saul was surrounded by a circle of brilliant young men who also honed their minds with intensely competitive verbal battles. First among these was Isaac Rosenfeld, who, at age thirteen and still in short pants, delivered an impressive lecture to the Tuley philosophy club on Nietzsche. Even less worldly than Saul, Isaac was universally admired for his grasp of complex ideas and for a remarkable capacity to convey them with clarity. From the moment Isaac stood up and opened his mouth, he and Saul became fast friends, drawn together by a shared desire to penetrate life's mysteries. Isaac went on to study philosophy at the University of Chicago and in graduate school at the University of Wisconsin. He also read fiction and shared Saul's ambition to write. Oscar Tarcov, a Tuleyite several years their junior, grew closer to Isaac and Saul after he arrived at the University of Chicago. Saul and Sam Freifeld were friends before they attended Tuley, but Sam's passion for philosophical ideas lacked the necessary level of intensity to be taken seriously by Saul, Oscar, and Isaac.

The Tuley crowd was also sophisticated in literary matters. Somehow able to procure a banned copy of James Joyce's *Ulysses*, Saul and his classmates quickly read the book and passed it from hand to hand. As soon as the ban on the book was lifted, a review was published in the school literary magazine, the *Tuley Review*.

Sydney Harris, later a syndicated columnist for Chicago newspapers, was a classmate who shared Saul's love of literature. They spent their free hours absorbing books, reading to one another, and writing at the Harrises' kitchen table. Mrs. Harris's tolerance extended beyond giving the boys a place to write. Sydney, showing off to his pal, talked back to his mother with a rudeness that shocked Saul, as it would have gotten him the back of my grandfather's hand. Eventually Saul and Sydney's love of writing produced a joint effort, a work of fiction they thought worthy of publication. They concocted a scheme: one of the boys would go to New York and get their book published. Sydney, the winner of the decisive coin flip, rode the rails east after swearing Saul to secrecy. Mrs. Harris was frightened by Sydney's disappearance and naturally was suspicious of Saul's complicity. Through the first round of questioning, Saul held his silence. However, after a few more days with no word, the police were brought in and Morrie, by now well connected to the Chicago police, seized the opportunity to terrorize his kid brother. Morrie told them that Saul was Sydney's friend, and the police grilled him so hard that he eventually gave up the missing boy's location. The book was never published, but the two remained friends and rivals for years. As high school graduation approached, Sydney confided to Rudy Lapp that Saul "did not have what it takes" to be a writer.

Saul joined the Tuley track team, an extension of his earlier effort to build up his physical strength. He trained by running around the lagoon in Humboldt Park. Even much later in his life, Saul still loved to run. In the late 1950s, he and I took to racing down Seventy-sixth Street in New York City. Beginning at the corner of West End Avenue, we'd start to sprint, skirting garbage cans, until we arrived, breathless, at the Tarcovs' at Riverside Drive. It wasn't until I was sixteen that I could beat him.

On one of Saul's visits to Rudy's, Mr. and Mrs. Lapp, thinking Saul could not understand Yiddish, spoke about his appearance. Mr. Lapp noted that Saul was handsome, to which Mrs. Lapp retorted that the devil was also handsome. Her comment stung Saul deeply, as he felt that Rudy's mother had seen evil in him. On a walk Saul and Rudy passed a streetside photo booth and Rudy decided they should have their picture taken. Saul, unhappy with how his likeness came out, scratched out his face. Rudy, whose nickel had paid for the photo, insisted on keeping it and retained the picture for more than sixty years. Decades later, Rudy still did not seem to understand that Saul had effaced himself from the picture out of wounded vanity.

Vanity was something the men in the Bellow family shared, as they thought themselves handsomer and smarter than everyone else. This perceived superiority was often their self-entitled rationale for bending or breaking rules that displeased them. While Sam tempered his feelings of entitlement, Abraham, Morrie, and Saul ignored social convention and viewed people who held contrary opinions with barely veiled contempt. My grandfather routinely dismissed objections with a backhand wave across his face, accompanied by the expression "feh," which meant, variously: I don't agree with you; you are wrong; you are ignorant; you are full of beans (or worse); end of discussion. But as his authority over his four nearly grown children slipped away, my grandfather redoubled his insistence on compliance by loudly demanding respect. In reaction, Morris and Saul rebelled openly, while Jane and Sam quietly did as they pleased.

Lescha was diagnosed with cancer in the late 1920s. Despite a mastectomy, my grandmother's cancer spread, and by 1932 it was clear that she was terminally ill. As his mother's strength ebbed, Saul would come directly home after high school to be with her. Once, she confided to him that her husband had turned away from her sexually. By way of explanation, she exposed the mastectomy scars on her chest. During Lescha's lingering illness, Abraham expressed unseemly interest in other women. When the shameful word got back to the family, Saul's anger about his father's disloyalty to his mother boiled over in a terrible argument between father and son, though I doubt either mind was changed.

In her last weeks, Grandma was bedridden and medicated with a narcotic drip. Saul portrayed her lingering illness and the heartbreak in the Bellow household in "Something to Remember Me By." The story ends after a young man successfully sneaks back into the house wearing a dress, the consequence of a prank played by his brother-in law's friends. Relieved not to be discovered, he is still greeted by a wordless smack when his father comes home, a sign of relief from a man whose terminally ill wife has survived one more day.

Lescha died in February 1933 at the age of fifty-three. At the funeral, Saul, seventeen and already harboring literary ambitions, eagerly engaged a family friend in the newspaper business in a conversation about writing. The guest, who thought Saul showed insufficient respect for his mother, expressed his disapproval to Abraham, who later lit into Saul, shaming him for putting his literary ambitions above his grief. Over the years Saul would introduce Lescha's early death into our frequent conversations about mortality with a grief as fresh as if he had just lost her.

Lescha's death removed the last constraint on the self-interest brewing in the now firmly established Bellow family. Openly citing his unfulfilled sexual needs, Abraham set about finding a new wife. Saul and Abraham were both on the prowl and Morrie was dating Marge. As the youngest, my father rarely got to use the sole family car for Saturday night dates. Grandpa soon married a recently widowed woman we called Aunt Fanny, and in Morrie and Marge's 1934 wedding photo Fanny sits in front

next to Abraham, holding the place of honor that Lescha
would have occupied. Morris, claiming his marriage to be
loveless, rationalized his choice by touting the investment capital
Marge brought to the match. Jane married a dentist and began
a family. Forced to abandon hopes of a medical career by his
father, Sam married and stayed in the coal business. Saul's version of Bellow family self-interest was to take another form,
his singular pursuit of writing.

Saul graduated from high school midyear and went to a junior college for one term. In the fall of 1933 he enrolled at the
University of Chicago and moved to nearby Hyde Park. Deeply
depressed, with a vague sense that academia was not what he
needed, Saul could not do much schoolwork. He read mostly
what pleased him, played pool in the Reynolds Club, and got
poor grades. In Hyde Park Saul met young people with unconventional attitudes and behaviors to match, including Beatrice
Freedman, who was affectionately called Beebee. Though my
father had yet to meet my mother, Beebee was the cousin and
childhood playmate of Saul's wife and would become a big part
of our lives.

Beebee was taken with romantic notions, unconventional
behavior, and a flair for the dramatic; she danced, painted, and
put her cash in the icebox because, after all, it was lettuce. Saul
loved to tell of a long conversation on the icy porch of her
boardinghouse where she, oblivious to the cold, stood in her
bare feet. He used that story, and others about her fruitless attempts to instill creative interests in her first husband, to show
how little attention Beebee paid to the real world. In later
years, when Saul became critical of women with excessively
romantic views, he called her a "fey girl," a pejorative term he

applied to women who affected imaginary notions to excess at the expense of reason.

Morrie and Marge moved to the South Side of Chicago, close to where Saul lived during the two years he spent at the university. Saul would come over to dinner and then retire to another room to read Whitman's *Leaves of Grass*. Marge was puzzled that Saul could spend so much time reading just *one* book. My father later said, "What was I supposed to do, go back into the other room and play gin rummy with Morrie and his political cronies?"

During Saul's sophomore year, one of the employees of the Carroll Coal Company was killed on the job. My grandfather had failed to pay his accident insurance premiums and the policy had lapsed, so the death caused a financial crisis that forced Saul to move home before his junior year. Depressed and without academic direction, Saul was floundering at the University of Chicago. On his long El rides to campus on the South Side, Saul went over Balzac or Tolstoy sentence by sentence to see if he could improve on them, often telling me that he was giving himself writing lessons that no academic training in literature could rival.

Adding to Saul's malaise was Abraham's open skepticism about of how his son's pursuit of literature might be put to a practical use. He pressured his youngest son to abandon college for the steady income of the coal business. When Saul resisted, Abraham derided him and his bookish friends with a vicious tongue. In a letter to Oscar Tarcov, Saul repeats Grandpa's claim to have read the great writers like Dostoyevsky and Tolstoy in Russian, but accuses him of not understanding the literary intent of fiction that was so important to Saul and his late-adolescent friends.

In preparation for a planned transfer to Northwestern in the fall of 1935, Saul took summer school courses at Chicago and continued to commute. For weeks he admired a beautiful young woman who also rode the El every morning before finally gathering the courage to approach her. A transfer student from the University of Illinois at Urbana, Anita Goshkin had moved home (after her father's death pinched her own family's finances) and was also commuting to summer school. Their first date included a swim in Lake Michigan near the university. That fall, Saul enrolled at Northwestern but continued to see Anita, who kept commuting to Hyde Park, where she quickly warmed to its atmosphere of left-wing political activity and to Saul's friends.

The Goshkin family had emigrated from Crimea after the pogroms that followed Japan's military victory over Russia in 1905. My maternal grandfather, Morris, left first and settled in Lafayette, Indiana, near members of his extended family. In 1908 my grandmother Sonia arrived at Ellis Island with their four children. My mother was born in 1914 and named Anita after Sonia's sister, a nurse who had died from an infected needle. Anita was a menopausal baby. When she was born, her brother Jack was nineteen, her sisters Catherine and Ida were sixteen and fourteen, respectively, while her brother Max was ten.

Morris's father, called Beryl Moshe by the family, lived in their home during Anita's first five years. Great-grandfather Goshkin had a big white beard and looked distinctly Asian, as did Morris and, to a lesser extent, Anita. His unworldly appearance and "old Russian" habits like spitting to ward off evil spirits made a deep impression on the imagination of Anita and her cousin Beebee, whose family lived nearby and visited often. An irritation to Sonia, who had to tolerate the spitting and keep a kosher home while he was alive, Beryl Moshe often went with Anita down the street to buy candy or to a nearby park. Because he was growing a little addled, Ida later joked that no one was sure who was taking care of whom, Beryl Moshe or four-year-old Anita.

Sonia Gadaskin Goshkin came from a family that educated its boys *and* girls. A woman with liberal ideas and a forceful personality, Sonia insisted that her children, particularly her daughters, pursue good educations. Her husband, Morris, was quiet, kind, and gentle. A milkman, he arose at 3:00 A.M. so he could deliver fresh dairy products to Lafayette households before breakfast. Later, the family milk business expanded to include an ice cream store. When Morris retired in 1931, my grandparents and Anita, aged sixteen, moved to Chicago, where several Goshkin children lived and where my grandfather would pass away three years later.

My uncle Jack married a woman named Ina while he was away at college and fathered a son, Jack Jr., my only Goshkin first cousin. But Sonia did not approve of Jack's gentile wife. Pressured by his domineering mother, Jack divorced Ina and returned to the family home after completing law school. He lived there for twenty years until he passed away from cancer in 1946, at fifty-one. Catherine and Ida attended college in the 1920s, and both later earned master's degrees in library science. So fierce was their independence that neither married. They proudly retained the title of "Miss Goshkin," correcting anyone who tried to address them with the politically correct "Ms." when that title came into fashion. Both worked in public libraries and enjoyed years of retirement in New York. Max became a machinist and lived in the family home until he married a piano teacher of great cultural pretension. Like Sonia, Esther Berger Goshkin ruled her household. She and Max moved to Los Angeles in the late 1940s, ostensibly for her health, but more likely because Esther wanted to substitute her influence on her husband for Sonia's.

During the summer of 1932, Anita's seventeenth year, the three sisters and their cousin Ethel took my uncle Jack's Hudson for an extended camping trip to as far west as Yellowstone Park. In the early years of the Depression, it was incredibly risky for four unaccompanied women to be driving around the country, let alone camping. Anita, one of two who could drive, took so much pride in the adventure that for the rest of her life she carried a picture in her wallet of the four campers in front of the Hudson.

Anita's family was filled with socialists and deeply committed to left-wing causes. She became involved with a Trotskyite circle at the University of Chicago and proudly told of the night she and Oscar Tarcov were arrested after a pro-union demonstration near a steel mill and spent a night in the Gary, Indiana, jail. In those days politics ruled every part of one's life, including one's love life. Oscar, a Trotskyite, dated a girl who belonged to a Stalinist group. Both factions ordered the romance terminated, and, after a final steak dinner, the couple complied.

According to Saul, Anita was the only woman to participate in Trotskyite debates until Celia Kaplan joined the group when she and her husband moved to Hyde Park in the early 1940s. Celia's husband, Harold "Kappy" Kaplan, told me that the men were interested in debating the fine points of theory, while

Anita always turned to the practical issue of direct action. De-cades later, when she took me to an admissions interview at the University of Chicago, my mother proudly led me to the spot in the lobby of the Social Science Building where she had sold more than one hundred copies of the Trotskyite magazine *Soapbox* in an hour. Saul wrote articles for the magazine.

By 1936 Saul and Anita were both living on the North Side of Chicago, dating frequently, and often dancing at the Aragon Ballroom on Lawrence Avenue. One Saturday night Saul bor-rowed the car and his father's suit. Quite a fuss ensued when the box of condoms Abraham found in his jacket pocket made it clear that Anita and Saul were having sex.

Saul hit his academic stride at Northwestern, where he com-pleted his B.A. cum laude with majors in English and anthro-pology, but he also got a taste of anti-Semitism in Evanston, where he was turned down for a date by a sorority girl because he was Jewish. There were few Jews on the Northwestern fac-ulty, but the anthropology department was a bit more open to them. Saul studied with Melville Herskovits, who supported his application to graduate school at the University of Wisconsin.

In the fall of 1937, Saul began graduate school in Madison, where he shared a room with Isaac Rosenfeld. During the few months he spent there, Saul sent his shirts home to be laun-dered by Aunt Fanny, who put five dollars in a shirt pocket before she sent them back. Saul was miserable. No doubt he missed Anita, who began her program at the School of Social Work at the University of Chicago that semester. Saul also fought with his father, who could understand college but drew the line at graduate study as an impractical waste of time and money. Mostly, Saul was disenchanted with anthropology. One of his professors recognized his passion for writing, commenting that his papers had the flavor of short stories rather than academic exercises. My father returned to Chicago for the Christmas break and never returned to Madison. Saul and Anita joined their friends Herb and Cora Passin and eloped on New Year's Eve, 1937. The double marriage ceremony was "festively" capped off by dinner in a Chinese restaurant. Isaac was charged with sending Saul's clothes and books back to Chicago.

Saul was beset with a dilemma. He did not want to comply with Abraham and go into the coal business, academia held no further interest, and he felt an intense desire, though it is hard to say exactly how well formed, to write. There is a hint of how early Saul had decided to fulfill his literary ambitions in his late novella, *The Actual*. At seventy-plus, Saul's central character, Harry Trellman, belatedly proposes to his high school sweetheart, seeking to correct what he now claims to be the error of rejecting the middle-class life Amy Wustrin represented. Amy, however, correctly reminds Harry that at eighteen he had convinced himself of the necessity of living an unconventional life in order to fulfill ambitions that were well enough established to overrule his affection for her.

Saul's choice to pursue a literary life was his version of the epidemic of self-interest that took over the Bellow family after Lescha's death. In contrast to the mutual sacrifices of family life in Lachine, I believe Saul came to feel that he and the Bellow family had lost the paradise of innocence after a decade of material success in Chicago.

The losses were multiple. First was his mother. Then his home: eighteen-year-old Saul could not live with his mercurial father and his new wife. But the most important loss was the absence of communal interest Lescha had engendered, a loss that was not fully apparent to Saul until Abraham's death twenty years later. While his father was alive, Saul still hoped to penetrate Abraham's mask of family civility and reach the love he sought. But what my father had hidden from himself was that his father hated his softness and vulnerability. When Grandpa died in 1955, my father's losses came to include the false innocence he had created as a young boy when he elevated a father brought low by failure to the status of a hero.

Nowhere is the loss of innocence clearer than in *Seize the Day*, which Saul wrote soon after his father's death. The narrator, Tommy Wilhelm, aspires to be an actor despite being ill suited to a profession where one must hide one's feelings behind the traditional theatrical mask. Dr. Adler, Tommy's father, is a better actor than his son—a man of consummate emotional control. A desperate Tommy makes one last desperate try to penetrate Dr. Adler's social façade and touch his heart by tearfully attributing the end of family life to his mother's death and by accusing Dr. Adler of feeling relief at her passing. Caught out in his lack of feeling, Dr. Adler still gives no quarter, offering only platitudes. Tommy, after failing once again to elicit a human response from his father, asks himself if he has falsely sentimentalized the past. Anticipating a future stripped of illusion, Tommy needs to mourn his compound losses and wanders into the funeral of a total stranger, a place where a grown man can cry freely.

Chapter Three

THE GYPSY LIFE WITH ANITA:
1938–43

LATE IN HER life, my mother counted the homes she had shared with Saul. Anita's total, twenty-two in their fifteen years together, stands in stark comparison with her two residences between Saul's departure in 1952 and her death in 1985.

Saul felt marriage should alter his status with Abraham. Not so his father. Soon after their wedding, Saul and Anita visited his father and Aunt Fanny. Saul said something that angered his father. As usual, Abraham raised his hand to strike his son, but Saul grabbed it in midair and said, "I'm a married man, Pa. You cannot hit me anymore." Grandpa did not hit Saul again. But Saul's marriage did not alter Abraham's rudeness. Following the polite custom among middle-class families, Abraham and Aunt Fanny invited Sonia and Catherine Goshkin and the newlyweds to a Sunday lunch. Most likely unhappy at his guests' liberal attitudes, Abraham finished eating and, without a word, rose from the table, retired to a nearby enclosed porch, and, in full sight of all, lay down, pulled a newspaper over his face, and went to sleep. The proper Goshkin women were stunned into silence by such ill-mannered behavior. Saul and Anita were mortified.

The newlyweds had no income and nowhere to live. Saul didn't have a job and Anita was a full-time student. They moved into the Goshkin home, and Saul briefly acceded to his father's pressure to work in the family coal business. According to Anita, he had to get up at the crack of dawn in freezing weather to go to work, and he soon quit in order to pursue writing. The already crowded Goshkin household was occupied by a widowed Sonia; Uncle Jack, who was practicing law; and my aunts, Catherine and Ida, who were librarians. In this lively place with distinct socialist leanings, Depression-era politics, philosophy, and literature were often debated.

Sonia supported the literary pursuits of her new son-in-law. Every morning, while Anita was at school and the others were at work, Saul wrote at a card table in a back room. He grew close to his mother-in-law, so close that my father was stung by her praise of his high school friend and rival Sydney Harris when Sydney published an article. Saul was full of envy then and remained so even at eighty-five, when he complained, "Your grandmother went on and on about what a success he was. There I was, brimming with talent, and Sonia kept going on about Harris." Oscar Tarcov speculated that Saul's affection for Sonia was so strong because he had recently lost his mother. Lescha had encouraged her son's scholarly aptitudes, and in her world that meant becoming a rabbi. I suspect Sonia's support of Saul's aspiration to write was similar to the way that Lescha might have acted.

After nine months, in the fall of 1938, Anita and Saul took an apartment in Hyde Park near Isaac and Vasiliki Rosenfeld, Sam and Rochelle Freifeld, Oscar and Edith Tarcov, Herb and Cora Passin, Hyman and Elaine Slate, and Beebee and Peter

Schenk. These friends and the neighborhood around the University of Chicago made for a stimulating intellectual atmosphere. Arguments between the Stalinists and the Trotskyites reached a peak, intensified by the Moscow show trials where Stalin consolidated his hold on the Communist Party. Hitler was becoming more bellicose and the Spanish Civil War pitted Franco against the Spanish Republican Army. Several of their friends joined the Lincoln Brigade, went to Spain, and were killed, bringing tears to Anita's eyes every time she remembered them.

Anita always found writing difficult, so Saul wrote most of her graduate school term papers. Daunted by the prospect of the thesis that a master's degree required, she did not complete the social work program. Anita took a job at the Chicago Relief Administration, where she gave out welfare checks in a South Side neighborhood for the then princely sum of twenty-five dollars a week. Both told me they were on easy street, because they could eat steak, at twenty-five cents a pound, whenever they wanted. Saul rented a small studio, where he wrote, and taught a few courses downtown at Pestalozzi-Froebel Teachers College. He took brief assignments for the WPA Writers Project and also worked on the Great Books of the Western World project at the University of Chicago. The editors kept shifting perspectives and Anita reported that he had to read *War and Peace* four times, each from a different point of view.

In *Shop Talk*, a book about writers and writing, Philip Roth portrays Saul's early literary development, particularly what my father considered the necessary step of moving beyond his roots. Roth describes how Saul was so enthralled by the great European literary masters—Balzac, Dostoyevsky, Kafka—that he sought distance from what he considered at the time to be the narrowing confines of Chicago, including his background as the son of a Jewish immigrant.

Saul also actively distanced himself from family traditions and made a point to the Bellows of Anita's status as a professional woman. The newlyweds were radicals who refused to observe formal religious practices and did not keep kosher. My aunt Marge described Abraham's agitated reaction after a visit to Saul and Anita's Hyde Park home. She and Morrie lived nearby and my grandfather stormed into their home, saying to Marge, "Cook me an egg in the shell," implying that this was all he could eat in their house, as they did not keep kosher either. As he ate the egg, Abraham expressed horror at having found a ham in my parents' icebox. Saul's defiance of family customs continued. Ten years later, while we were living in Minneapolis, Saul visited Chicago on the Jewish High Holiday Yom Kippur. To the chagrin of all the Bellows except Sam, Saul borrowed the family car and drove to the South Side to visit his friends, while the rest of the family, as prescribed by Jewish law, walked to the synagogue and prayed.

My father's desire to write continued to mystify Abraham, who could more easily understand Morrie's outstripping him in business than Saul's pursuit of an impecunious life devoted to culture. Decades later, after my aunt Jane fell asleep in the front row at his Nobel lecture, Saul complained bitterly on the way back to the hotel that she typified the family's attitude toward his devotion to culture.

While my parents claimed not to care about social convention, they were not completely immune. On a visit to the

Goshkin home Oscar Tarcov, Saul, and Anita were eating a watermelon on the porch and spitting the seeds into a neighbor's yard. Later that night, Saul had to go over to collect them on his hands and knees in the dark before the irritable neighbor complained to my grandmother about the mess.

A smoldering 1937 picture of Anita and Saul, cherished for the rest of their lives by both, shows how beautiful my parents were. But it did not take long for Saul to develop a taste for sex outside of marriage. As part of their left-wing political belief system, Saul and Isaac Rosenfeld adopted a belief that fidelity was a bourgeois ideology. It was just like the two men to draw an ideological cloak around their infidelities. When Hyman Slate visited my father in his writing studio in 1939, as they walked up the stairs Saul warned Hyman that he had a girl stashed there and asked him to keep it from Anita.

Saul was now well able to construct rationales to justify his sexual behavior. But his feelings toward women were grounded, I believe, in deeply maternal forms of love like that I find in the selfless, protective love of Grandma Lescha. Whether or not Saul actually received uncritical acceptance from his mother, or merely wished for it, is an unanswerable question buried in the past. A bit more tangible are stories he told about Lescha's ability to inspire compassion, to soften Abraham's temper, and to understand the human heart.

Mitzi McClosky, loyal wife of the often-critical Herb, exemplifies that kind, good-hearted woman. A friend for sixty years, she dearly loved Saul and he returned her affections. His telling Yiddish description of her to a mutual friend was *"Sie hat keine biene,"* which translates as "She has no bones"—that is, no hardness.

The selfless, unspoken love of a mother for a son comes through in *The Adventures of Augie March* and *Herzog*. Though barely able to communicate outside of her home, Mrs. March possesses an unerring intuition about people that is readily apparent to her son Augie. And the palpable love of Mother Herzog is captured in her last moments as she strokes Moses's hand with fingers that have turned blue.

The protective love of women is often tacit and so subtle in Saul's writing as to be easily missed. In the short story "What Kind of Day Did You Have?" Victor Wulpy's mistress Katrina Goliger puts the welfare of her children at risk as she drops everything just to be with Victor because he is anticipating an unpleasant controversy with an intellectual adversary. Katrina makes herself available emotionally and sexually just to suit Victor's transient moods and needs. Only as the story ends does the self-preoccupied Victor even pause long enough to inquire after her by asking the question that forms the story's title. In the short story "Cousins," Saul's narrator, Ijah Brodsky, catalogs the help he has offered family throughout a lifetime marked by having taken no support in return until he quietly slips his arm into that offered by a strong young female cousin who notices a momentary flicker of physical weakness in him.

Saul battled with his tender sentiments over a lifetime, but I cannot be certain how clearly he saw them as an essential aspect of himself. However, he knew that the softness he sought from women was central to his happiness. Perhaps most clearly illustrated in his letters, his need for comfort from a woman when he felt alone, bereft, or anxious could overpower his logic, his common sense, and his memory of previous errors in judgment. Fifteen years after their bitter divorce, he frantically called Sasha, his second wife, at work the day after being awarded the Nobel Prize. Incredibly, he sought *her* solace for the burdens that winning the prize placed on him!

Saul, who described himself as a serial monogamist, sought more than a lover or even an unending series of them could offer. For reasons no doubt unclear to him at the time, Saul married women who possessed some measure of the hardness that I see as necessary to be able to take care of him. Though he took little initial note of the constraint that accompanies such strengths, Saul became acutely aware of them and chafed when each wife, in turn, exerted her will, causing various forms of conflict that were severe enough to sour his first four marriages.

No single factor can explain Saul's sexual exploits, during and between his marriages. High on my list of causes is competition, particularly with his brother Morrie, who turned his own extramarital conquests into a public spectacle by keeping a second household, complete with children. Saul's intellectual competition with his peers certainly extended to their seduction of women. There was lust, of course, but also the boost to Saul's vanity that came when women expressed sexual interest in him. Success with new women helped restore Saul's prowess and self-esteem after his second and third marriages failed.

Countless women were taken by Saul's humor, charm, and great physical beauty, and he was frequently on the receiving end of their attention. Saul never said a word, but I have been told repeatedly that women made their sexual interest apparent and often went so far as to throw themselves at him. *The Adventures of Augie March* offers a nonerotic explanation for why women found the title protagonist irresistible that very much applies to Saul. During Augie's late teens, the Renlings, a wealthy childless couple, take a liking to the handsome lad. Throughout the novel, Augie repeatedly, though briefly, allows himself to be shaped by the desires of others, and Mrs. Renling sees in him a young man she can tutor and guide. Augie, musing about his appeal, characterizes himself as adoptable, a word that suggests my father communicated a hint of softness and pliability that drew out protective feelings in women along with the illusion that they could shape Saul into what they wanted him to be.

Anita also subscribed to the ideology of sexual liberation, at least in name. Saul, defending his own conduct, said Anita came home once or twice and announced in what he described as a mechanical tone that she had slept with this or that communist comrade. Her lack of emotion made me wonder if, rather than feeling passion, she was just trying to impress upon Saul the consequences of his infidelities. Anita had chosen one comrade in particular to make him jealous. She likely hoped to hurt Saul and provoke him into stopping the pain he was causing her. But Anita, a stoic and an ideologue, never complained or admitted to me how hurt she was by Saul's infidelities.

Infidelity almost ended my parents' marriage in 1940 during their three months in Mexico. A windfall of five hundred dollars from an insurance policy on Lescha's life financed the trip. My father was the beneficiary, but Abraham demanded the money for the coal business. Saul refused. He wanted to go to Europe, but World War II made that journey impossible, so he and Anita boarded a bus for Mexico, which was then home to the exiled Leon Trotsky and a haven for expatriates from around the globe. In Taxco, Saul and Anita frequented a lively cantina, where they danced and Saul drank a good deal. During their first few weeks, my father took off with another woman for several days. Angered, and knowing Saul's vulnerability to public shame, Anita retaliated by having a public affair. The only time Anita ever mentioned it, she told me her lover was a very handsome Mexican. A nasty fight ensued when Saul returned, and Anita went to Acapulco by herself for a few days. Herb and Cora Passin joined my parents after they had been in Taxco for a month. While the two couples shared a house, Herb and Cora saw no signs of discord. Both Saul and Anita, no doubt chastened, had decided to paper over the infidelities, a solution that lasted a decade and brought me into the world. But Saul was intoxicated by the idea of freedom in Mexico, and the seeds of his discontent with my mother had been planted.

Herb and Saul, both admirers of Trotsky, arranged to meet with him in Mexico City through the intercession of a Chicago friend. The day before the scheduled meeting, Trotsky was murdered by a Stalinist agent. In the postmortem confusion, Herb and Saul went to the morgue and, mistaken for American journalists, were allowed in to view the corpse. Both men were deeply affected by seeing Trotsky, whose head was still wrapped in bandages and streaked with blood and iodine.

When Saul and Anita returned to Chicago in the fall of 1940, the war in Europe was raging. Anita went to work at Michael Reese Hospital. Saul wrote and taught part-time. In the early 1940s the *Partisan Review*, a magazine based in New York and run by a circle of left-wing intellectuals, published several of my father's short stories. By then Isaac Rosenfeld, having left graduate school in Madison, had moved to Greenwich Village. Isaac and Saul, two Chicagoans who shared a passion for literature and left-wing politics, were welcomed into what my mother called the "*PR* crowd." Saul's *Partisan Review* colleagues believed his talents as a writer made him the best candidate to counter the prevalent anti-Semitism in American literary and academic hierarchies. Saul later maintained that the magazine was primarily political. At the *PR* office, he once overheard the editor Philip Rahv on the phone with a fellow editor, who was inquiring if any worthwhile submissions had arrived. Rahv replied, "No, nothing interesting, just fiction."

Anita, whose job curtailed her ability to travel, remained in Chicago, but Saul, excited by his *Partisan Review* connections and the freedom of New York, began to make regular visits there. On our frequent walks around the Village during the early 1960s, Saul used to point out places where he had stayed years earlier, omitting the women he no doubt saw on those trips.

My father was at loose ends in Chicago during most of World War II. He had to have a hernia operation in order to be healthy enough to join the military. However, the entire Bellow family lacked U.S. citizenship, which prevented Saul from joining the service and Morrie from taking the bar exam. A friend of Anita's who worked at the Immigration Department helped the Bellow family resolve the problem caused by its illegal entry fifteen years earlier. Saul had to return to Canada and reenter the country legally. He later told me that Anita and her friend's success with the family's immigration status "made his stock go up in the Bellow household."

Saul's narrator in *Dangling Man*, his first published novel, is at loose ends as well. Looking toward an ill-defined future, an increasingly alienated Joseph finds himself at odds with family, friends, neighbors, and even a wife who is growing more independent of him. Plagued by paralytic doubts, he dangles between

the job he has quit and the army, which he hopes to join. Whatever personal insecurities my father may have felt as he dangled
in the early 1940s did not stop him, an unknown Jewish novelist, from throwing down the gauntlet to the American literary
establishment personified by Ernest Hemingway. In the first
pages of *Dangling Man*, published in 1944, Saul advocated rede-
fining heroism as resulting not from outer accomplishments
achieved in distant battle but rather from the inner world of
thought, reflection, and emotional turmoil. According to Anita,
Saul and his friends would read Hemingway out loud, deriding
his spare and choppy prose. Given Saul's eventual impact on
American fiction, his first published paragraphs, about the cen-
trality of what my father called the "inner life," contain a literary
prophecy. My father's strong critical sensibility already extended to his own work. When John Howard Griffin published
Black Like Me in 1961, Anita told me that during the mid-1940s
Saul had written a novel entitled *The Very Dark Trees*, in which
a white man wakes up black. Saul was dissatisfied with the manuscript and burned it. Only years later did I learn that his novel
had been favorably received by a potential publisher. Saul must
have had a lot of faith in himself to burn *The Very Dark Trees*.

Chapter Four

OUR GYPSY LIFE ENDS: 1944–51

M Y 1944 BIRTH was harrowing. I became detached
from the placenta and Anita had to have an emergency
cesarean. Saul did not know if either of us would live through
my first night. Every April 16 my father repeated the story of
my birth: the heroic Dr. Koffman who saved our lives, the cold
and drizzly sky that greeted a much-relieved Saul as he walked
over to Beebee's, and the breakfast of a dozen fried eggs she
cooked him.

From the time I was an infant, Saul thought that the upper
half of my face resembled the Bellow side of the family, while
the bottom half resembled the Goshkins. My baby book is replete with revealing comments in Anita's hand about my father
taking an active role, as neither parent wanted me to become a
"mama's boy." As soon I could chew solids, Saul insisted on
feeding me pickled herring. After I could understand direc-
tions, he involved me in his irreverent sense of humor. Saul
would say, "Gregory, point to your ass." When I did so, he followed with "Point to your elbow," and would break into gales
of laughter as he said, "Now you know more than a Harvard
graduate."

As World War II came to an end, Saul was finally able to join the merchant marine. Anita and I lived with the Goshkins during the six months he was stationed in Brooklyn and Baltimore. Saul spent most of his free time reading in the Baltimore public library, which he preferred to visiting what his fellow sailors called "Clapp Hill." Saul was given a psychiatric examination because he refused officers' training despite a high IQ. When the psychiatrist asked about his interests, Saul said he was reading about John Dewey's theory of pragmatism. The psychiatrist's notes, which Saul read when the doctor left the room (perhaps purposefully), indicated that my father's lack of purpose disqualified him from being an officer. Saul was so deeply wounded by the psychiatrist's comments that years later, he had his narrator Moses Herzog address a letter to a Dr. Zozo, candidly telling his psychiatric examiner of the anguish he had caused in an uncannily similar incident.

Immediately after his discharge, Saul decided on a move to New York. We stored our furniture in the basement of a hotel Morrie owned. Through Alfred Kazin he met Arthur Lidov, a painter whose wife, Vicki, Saul had known since his undergraduate years. They had been living in Brooklyn but had decided on a move to the country. Anita, Saul, and I joined them in upstate New York during a bitterly cold winter. Just as the adults thought they had succeeded in warming up the house, they looked down at two-year-old me toddling closer to the floor and could see my breath. Vicki told me my parents' relationship was very physically passionate. But that did not deter Saul from openly seeing other women when he went down to New York to teach at NYU. Arthur made a sketch of my father hitchhiking as an available woman passes by riding a bull, which captures

Saul's passive yet eager availability to engage in extramarital sexual liaisons. Even after eight years of a marriage plagued by infidelities, Anita tolerated Saul's affairs, telling herself and Vicki that he was still sowing his wild oats.

We returned to New York City, but by the fall of 1947 we were off to Minneapolis, where Herb McClosky helped my father get a job in the humanities department of the University of Minnesota. Eric Bentley, who became a distinguished theater critic, was also invited there by Joseph Warren Beach, the department chairman who attracted talented young faculty members with a small teaching load that allowed time to write. As late as the late 1940s, academic departments of English would not hire Jews, who were presumed incapable of understanding great literature, let alone creating it. The systemic exclusion of Jews angered Saul, and Mitzi McClosky described how his nostrils flared at even a hint of that pervasive anti-Semitism. But Saul frequently described his early novels, *Dangling Man* and *The Victim*, as his M.A. and Ph.D. My father's point was that he was self-taught as a writer and that academia had little to offer him. Yet he was still writing in a style largely shaped by the same scholars who had rejected Jewish writers, trying, I believe, to prove his worth to them.

Our domestic life in Minneapolis began with residing in a Quonset hut—basically half of a large inverted tin can with no insulation. The two families it housed were separated by a barrier of sheet metal. The heating was terrible and, according to Anita, we had to choose between the half with a kitchen sink and the half with a toilet. We chose the side with the sink because, she said, "at least you could pee in a sink." Grandpa Abraham visited us in Minneapolis but stayed with the McCloskys, as the Quonset hut was unsuitable. Every day, dressed in a suit and tie, he sat at their dining room table, though he refused to eat their nonkosher food, and regaled Herb and Mitzi with boastful stories about the financial success of his other children.

We lived in a large house during our second year in Minneapolis and rented a room to Max Kampelman, a conscientious objector during World War II who had just been discharged. Max's alternative service was to participate in a study of human survival, recently described by Todd Tucker in *The Great Starvation Experiment*. Max had had to live on a minimal number of calories and was so thin that Anita said he looked as if he had been in a concentration camp. She joked about his raiding the icebox at all hours.

Anita and Eric Bentley's beautiful young wife, Maja, were faculty wives who took care of the everyday details of life for their creative husbands. Anita and Mitzi also became friends, and I was frequently at the McClosky house playing with Jane, Herb and Mitzi's daughter. According to Mitzi, at four o'clock, Saul would excuse himself from campus activities to "go home and play with my kid." He entertained me while Anita made dinner.

Our house became a social center where my increasingly gregarious father brought people over at all hours. Saul entertained visitors with jokes, stories, and readings from drafts of *The Victim*. Anita did her best to accommodate the guests, often feeding large numbers of people with no forewarning. Eventually, she became irked with entertaining and bored by hearing the same stories and jokes. Just as Saul got to a punch line, Anita would show her frustration by interrupting him to say the garbage needed to be taken out. According to Mitzi, Saul's chronic philandering finally became an increasing irritant to my mother. As a way to undermine his running around, Anita cultivated friendships with the women who showed interest in her husband.

As part of his development as a writer, Saul thought it necessary to move away from his cultural and religious roots. He rejected religious practice and custom, but his identification as a Jew was apparent in his resentment of the anti-Semitic biases in academia. And, according to Anita, if pushed too hard in an argument, Saul's fallback position was to accuse his opponent of anti-Semitism.

The anti-Semitism embedded in New York's literary and critical hierarchies permeates his 1948 novel, *The Victim*. In a crucial scene, a magazine editor refuses to consider hiring the narrator, Asa Leventhal, a Jewish job applicant with moxie. During the interview a nasty argument ensues after the busy editor gruffly asks Asa why he applied for a job without the requisite background, a broad allusion to Asa's Jewish roots.

A similar scene occurred between my father and Whittaker Chambers, then arts and literature editor at *Time* magazine, who turned Saul down for a job. During the interview they had a heated dispute about Romantic poets. Saul often repeated the story, although he did not describe their literary disagreement or bring up the editor's anti-Semitism. More than once he said the reason for Chambers's rejection was his envy of Saul's good looks.

Leaving the contentious job interview, Asa, Saul's narrator, also fumes. But in *The Victim*, which I consider my father's most optimistic novel, even a subject as dark as anti-Semitism does not alter "young Saul's" benign view of human nature. The images of harmony and reconciliation with which Saul ends the novel convince me that my father's optimism still prevailed in 1948. Several times he mentioned that the theme of reconciliation received scant critical attention, but his tolerance and universal humanism resonate with me because they were the prevalent values in our household. I find a confirming residue of Saul's utopian hopes in a letter to Oscar Tarcov that contains a comment about meeting the world's material needs as a prelude that will "enable *Hamlet*." I believe Saul refers to the Trotskyite idealism he and Oscar shared a decade earlier: that in order for the appreciation of culture to be more than a luxury for mankind, a new world order must first provide food and shelter.

In 1980, in Chicago to celebrate Saul's sixty-fifth birthday, I learned a bit more about Saul's youthful optimism. My father and I were taking a walk and encountered the aged Nathan Leites, who greeted us stiffly on the street and then passed on. As we continued walking, Saul told me that he was the former professor who, forty-five years earlier, greeted him in Hyde Park with the friendly question "How is the *romancier*?" Even decades later, Saul remained mystified that Leites could have so mischaracterized him as a romantic. To the contrary, I was mystified that my father could not see, or could no longer see, that his youthful idealism had been readily apparent to his teacher.

By 1948 Saul had published two novels, but his sales were minuscule and did not generate enough money to live on. But my father was granted a one-year Guggenheim Fellowship that enabled us to go to Paris for a year. The three of us squeezed into a tiny cabin on a broken-down tub named the *De Grasse*. Saul chose

Paris because of its literary and cultural history. Cold, dreary, and uninviting, postwar Paris was nothing like what he imagined. A biting wind or a pea-soup fog made my walks to school miserable. Saul's constant run-ins with landlords and bureaucrats reminded him of Dostoyevsky's accounts of life in Paris. When I was ill, my father sought permission to buy an extra ration of coal from the Parisian authorities. After filling out numerous forms, the clerk would not approve the request because the perforations on the doctor's authorization form were on the wrong side. My father, angered at a useless bureaucratic exercise, threatened to buy the coal on the black market. The clerk merely shrugged.

But Anita did not want to leave Minneapolis. Our gypsy lifestyle was wearing on her. She wanted to settle down and have another child. Somewhere in Europe, frustrated by too many moves, she went on strike, planting her bottom on our trunks and refusing to go to our next destination. Saul had to move the luggage and carry my intransigent mother as well.

American money went far in postwar Paris, and we lived in relative comfort. But daily life was a physical challenge. All three of our apartments during the time in Paris were coal heated, and there was no refrigeration. Shopping was a daily or even twice-daily matter; Anita would go out with her *filet*, or net, to shop, and then return to cook our next meal. Fresh milk was hard to come by, but we had access to the military PX, where we bought dreadful-tasting powdered milk. Anita resorted to adding cocoa to make the mixture more palatable, although a repellent scum still formed as soon as it cooled. My parents hired a maid named Augusta to cook, clean, and look after me. She came to her job interview immaculately dressed but showed up to work in carpet slippers and hair curlers, and minus her false teeth. Augusta made me sit in the stairwell while my parents were out, and they fired her after I told them. Lillian Bodnia, a Danish Jew who had hidden with her family during the Holocaust, became my nanny. She and I cut and pasted hearts and made long chains of colored paper ovals, and she introduced me to stamp collecting.

Anita did not want me to begin first grade in a French public school, so I spent an extra year in a private bilingual kindergarten. I was already shy, and our frequent moves made it worse. The few children among my parents' friends were my only playmates. Surrounded by adults, I became proficient at amusing them. My imitation of Americans trying to speak French was a big hit. I roller-skated in the Tuileries and liked to jump over the fences and run in the grass. However, I was poorly coordinated and fell so often that I acquired the nickname "Tomato Knees," as they were always painted in red Mercurochrome. Years later, on a visit to Paris, I was surprised to see how low the barriers around the lawns in the Tuileries actually are.

Paris was teeming with young American expatriates, among them Herbert Gold, Truman Capote, and James Baldwin, whose apartment had no shower. Baldwin came over regularly to use ours, usually showing up around dinnertime, Saul wryly noted. Saul and Jesse Reichek, a young American painter, used to meet after work in a café and play casino over beer in the summer and hot cocoa in the winter. Several Chicago friends, including Julian Behrstock and Harold "Kappy" Kaplan, who worked for the U.S. State Department, now lived there. But even friendships held little cheer for a very depressed Saul during our early months in a dreary Paris.

I learned about how Saul's mood was intertwined with a literary dilemma from the letters he wrote years later to Philip Roth, which Roth published right after my father died. Saul was stuck on a novel with a morbid theme titled *The Crab and the Butterfly*. Though abandoned and never published, the novel reveals the literary breakthrough brewing within my father. It centers on two men: one is in a hospital dying while the other urges him to cling to life. The death of one character and the survival of the other, I think, reflect two parts of Saul Bellow, a novelist in transition. The character who dies is the part of Saul that clung to the familiar, though doomed, academic fictional forms of his European "mentors." The survivor is the writer with a freewheeling style of writing who was about to burst forth in the pages of *The Adventures of Augie March*.

As this struggle was going on within, Saul was walking down the street watching merchants hose fruit and vegetables that had gone bad into the Seine, ridding themselves of once useful commodities that had lost their value and creating tiny rainbows of water in the gutter. At that very moment, the first lines of *The Adventures of Augie March* poured out of him as if they had been sitting there for a long time. Saul Bellow threw out *his* garbage—ending his literary apprenticeship by abandoning a fictional style designed to please academics in favor of a naturally flowing prose style that signaled a breakthrough in American literature.

Saul's grant money was running out after our first year, but Anita now did not want to leave Paris. My father later maintained that going back to the States meant "facing the music" about ending a marriage they both knew could not survive. In order to support our second year, Anita got a job at Joint Distribution, where she was to find adoptive parents for Jewish orphans who still had no homes four years after the war. I recall sitting in long, frightening hallways when my mother had no choice but to take me on a last-minute visit to an orphanage.

With a novel that seemed to be writing itself, Saul's dark mood and demeanor changed radically. He became a jauntily dressed young man about town who participated in a free-spirited café life with writers, painters, and intellectuals. Saul and Kappy Kaplan readily took to these Parisian circles. Both men maintained that they should explore all that life had to offer, including adopting the French tolerance of infidelity as yet another rationale. Fashioning himself an unofficial cultural attaché, Kappy threw large parties where my father often met women who were attracted to him and did not see his marriage as an obstacle to sleeping with him. Soon Anita refused to accompany him, and finally grew intolerant of Saul's now epic philandering. My parents would rarely complain about each other to friends, but Saul's sexual roving got so bad that Anita openly commiserated with Celia Kaplan, who suffered even more deeply from her own husband's open sexual liaisons. A particularly sore point was a serious affair Saul had with a woman named Nadine, whom he had met at one of Kappy's parties. Nadine had been Kappy's lover at the time, and threw him over for Saul. The men fell out over it, and Anita, claiming Celia was responsible for introducing Saul to Nadine, ended their friendship, wounding a close friend with a false accusation.

That affair became a tipping point between Anita and Saul, but according to Herb Gold, Saul had women stashed all over town. In the late 1980s, I spent a week in Paris with my father. During my stay Kappy explained the mores that had prevailed in their youth, which included classifying lovers as first-, second-, and third-tier in emotional, but not sexual, priority. On that visit a belatedly chastened Saul told me how guilty he felt about his behavior forty years earlier, saying "I can't walk around a corner without thinking of the pain I caused your mother." But indulging so fully in the sexual freedom Saul found in Paris was just a symptom of the sad state of my parents' marriage. Anita had had her fill of the gypsy lifestyle. My elementary school education could no longer be postponed, so we left Europe. But by then the marriage was doomed.

Before returning to the United States, we took a grand cultural tour of Europe. Saul taught at the Salzburg Seminar in American Studies, which was housed in the Schloss Leopoldskron. I had the run of a castle filled with suits of armor on the landings. It was heaven for a six-year-old boy. I recall playing in a marshy area dotted with statues of sea horses, which I joyfully rode. A very young Ted Hoffman, who became a longtime friend of Saul's, ran the seminar in an informal way. Eric Bentley was also there with his wife, Maja. Fluent in English and German, Maja got a job with the U.S. government's occupying forces, which required travel between Salzburg and Vienna, a city still cordoned off by Russian troops. When our month was over Maja took Anita and me to Vienna in her car. I was curled up on the backseat in the middle of the night when we were stopped by Russian soldiers. Flashlights shone in my face and I was terrified, but Maja's U.S. papers got us through, and I remember the performance of *The Magic Flute* we saw in Vienna.

During a brutally hot summer, we spent a month in Rome living above a pasta shop where large sheets of dough were hung up to dry before being cut into spaghetti. The odor of *latterias*, milk and cheese shops, carried for blocks. Bored stiff, Anita and I often went to Rome's zoo, which featured a pink-skinned newborn baby elephant and a bicycle-riding chimp named Gregorio, my name in Italian. By then I had seen dozens of churches. When Saul tried to pique my flagging interest by telling me St. Peter's was the biggest church in the world, I responded, "In that case we don't need to see any more!"

Our final Italian stop was Positano, a town on the Amalfi coast noted for its beauty. Every morning for six weeks, while Saul wrote, Anita and I descended a long staircase to the beach, where she taught me to swim. Our daily routine included a siesta after lunch and a late-afternoon walk to the main part of town, where we feasted on freshly made mozzarella Anita said tasted sweeter than ice cream. One afternoon my parents miscommunicated and I was left alone at the town's only intersection. I remained perfectly calm and walked home as my parents panicked. On our drive back to Paris, it was my turn to panic. We stopped for ice cream, and when I finished before the others, I climbed into my father's lap. Bronzed by daily swimming and without a haircut for weeks, I must have looked like an urchin trying to beg money from the rich Americans. A white-helmeted officer tried to shoo me away and, after failing to dislodge me from Saul's lap, he threatened to arrest me. Saul said "He's my son" in Italian, but the policeman thought my father was just trying to protect a beggar. Finally, the waiter confirmed that I had arrived with the adults and the officer went on his way.

When we returned from Europe, we spent a month in Chicago. By now Anita and Saul were barely speaking, and both complained openly to family and friends as never before. They were dead broke, but Saul's manuscript *of Augie March* was far enough along to attract the interest of Harold Guinzburg, publisher of the Viking Press, who helped us rent an apartment in Forest Hills, a neighborhood in Queens, New York.

In September of 1950 I began at P.S. 175, where the school day for first graders ended at noon. If my mother was late, I often cried. One day, late because she had waited for Saul to finish writing, Anita brought him along to pick me up. I was already in tears. Recognizing my father's ability to cheer me up, she said, "Look who came to pick you up from school." But Anita had to earn a salary and got a job at a Planned Parenthood clinic in Far Rockaway that prevented her from picking me up at noon. Saul and Anita sought advice about a suitable school from Rachel and Paulo Milano, friends who lived nearby. Their son Andy attended a private school that offered a full academic day supplemented by what my mother called "after-school supervision." In practice that meant simply letting the kids with working parents have the run of the school and its playground until they were picked up.

The Queens School was populated by red-diaper babies, a term used to describe the children of communists. It was run along lines so egalitarian that we called adults by their first names and once locked our teacher out of the classroom after "going on strike." The learning model was based on the progressive educational philosophy of John Dewey, which included studying a single theme in depth for a whole school year. I remember that we built a working model of the solar system; made a huge plywood copy of the New York City transit system and took a field trip to see how the subway works; and

studied all the American Indian tribes, even fabricating miniature birch-bark canoes. The school was racially integrated;
among its black students were the sons of the Brooklyn Dodger
greats Jackie Robinson and Roy Campanella, who chose it because their all-white neighborhood schools had turned them
away. Everything was freely discussed. Saul, on a visit to our classroom, watched as my class used sex to divert the teacher from a
math lesson. As she began, one of us would raise a hand and ask
what *fuck* meant. After carefully outlining the mechanics of
sexual intercourse, the teacher tried to return to the lesson, only
to be derailed by a variation of the same question—a process
that ended only at recess.

Permissive attitudes also prevailed in our home. My table
manners were nonexistent by the time we returned from Europe. In Italy, I developed a fondness for eating spaghetti by
twirling it around my fork to form a big ball and working my
way up the thin strands. It was a great hit with waiters but very
messy. Soon we were invited to dinner by our new Forest Hills
neighbors. To their chagrin, my habit of eating chocolate pud-
ding with my fingers elicited nary a word from either parent. In
conscious contrast to his father, Saul took pride in not hitting
me and made a point of telling me so. Yet, while I had no physical
fear of my father, his tongue was withering when he was angry.
As a young mother, Anita attended the child psychoanalyst
Bruno Bettelheim's workshops and adopted many of his child-
rearing ideas. One was that sweets should not be used as a reward.
I remember plates of candy in our apartment that I barely touched
because they were there all the time. During my adolescence,
Anita's permissiveness extended to leaving cigarettes out; my
friends loved to come over and smoke them.

In 1951 *The Adventures of Augie March* and Ralph Ellison's *Invisible Man* were nearing completion. We spent a good deal of time with Ralph and Fanny Ellison at our apartment and vacationing on Long Island, where Saul, Ralph, and I went fishing. Anita told me that writing *Invisible Man* took so much out of Ralph that when he finished, he got into bed for weeks, convinced that he was going to die. Ralph had a number of talents that included electronics; as a birthday gift for Saul, Anita had him put together a Heathkit hi-fi system. My parents tested it by playing Laurence Olivier's recording of *Hamlet* with the volume turned up. Frightened by Olivier's ominous tones, I fled our apartment, bounding down the stairs. A neighbor, alarmed by the noise, came out and asked me if anything was wrong. I told her, "I am up to *here* with Shakespeare!"

I was an awkward kid and had so much trouble learning to ride a bike that for weeks Saul ran along with his hand on the seat to steady me. Shy and with few friends because I didn't go to the neighborhood school, I rarely went beyond the sidewalk in front of our apartment. On one of my rare solo excursions, I was threatened by several bullies. After I pointed them out to Saul, he threatened to beat them up if they ever bothered me again—which they did not. Before I went to bed, Saul read Joseph A. Altsheler's heroic tales of Henry Ware's frontier adventures aloud to me. Anita and I chuckled for years because Saul became so caught up in the stories that he continued reading long after I had fallen asleep. Flush with money after the publication of *Augie March*, Saul bought me a pogo stick, a sleeping bag, and stilts for my ninth birthday. "These are things I wanted as a kid but we couldn't afford them," he said. The pogo stick didn't last long, but I walked around the apartment on the stilts for years.

After a year or two in Forest Hills, Saul could no longer tolerate the stable domestic life in our middle-class neighborhood.
When he was leaving the building wearing a seersucker suit, the
height of style among Americans in Paris, a neighbor asked Saul
if he was going fishing. At a party to celebrate the publication of
Augie March, another neighbor complained of the noise and my
father threatened to push him down the incinerator chute.

No doubt partly because he was disenchanted with Anita
and our increasingly conventional lifestyle, Saul followed Isaac
Rosenfeld into Reichian analysis. A fringe version of psychoanalysis based on Wilhelm Reich's late-career ideas about cos-
mic energy and heightening sexual gratification, Saul began
therapy with Dr. Chester Rayfield. Dr. R., as my parents called
him, practiced in Forest Hills. According to Saul, Reichian
technique emphasized breaking down intellectual resistance
to maximize the power of the body and emotion. In the middle
of the winter with the window wide-open, Saul lay on the couch
in his underwear while Dr. R., wearing an overcoat, characterized his bodily postures as defenses and encouraged him to express his bestial impulses. Roaring like a lion became a favorite
activity that he and I continued for years whenever a loud subway train pulled into our station.

We had an orgone box, a device designed to capture and
intensify celestial energy. About the size of a telephone booth
and lined with Brillo pads, it occupied a niche in the hallway.
Isaac and Vasiliki Rosenfeld had a two-seater in their tiny Bar-
row Street apartment. Perhaps because adults went into it nude,
at seven I grasped its purpose and sat in it for long, uninterrupted
masturbatory sessions that neither permissive parent thought
to stop.

Hoping to save her marriage, Anita went to Dr. R. for a few visits and must have placed great faith in the therapist's opinion. Sixty years later I still shudder when I recall Anita's plaintive tone as she asked Saul about Dr. R.'s view on some matter. My mother hoped in vain. Dr. R.'s assessment was that Anita's character was too rigid. He advocated a divorce. Reichian analysis merely confirmed Saul's opinion that Anita was an unsuitable wife and supported his complaints about her narrowness and controlling nature.

Anita was the major family breadwinner and kept a series of envelopes in her dresser drawer, neatly labeled and filled with the money needed to pay each bill. As their marriage deteriorated, my father was dismayed to find an envelope labeled "Saul" in her dresser, as if he were just another expense. For decades Saul used his horror at finding that envelope to justify the divorce to me. Years later, as my father repeated the story about using his windfall from Lescha's insurance policy to finance my parents' 1940 trip to Mexico, I asked how exactly he had spent the five hundred dollars. After decades of complaint about Anita and her envelopes, Saul sheepishly confessed that he had turned the cash over to her.

Saul and Anita slept in separate rooms for many months while he vacillated about leaving for good. Anita's enthusiasm for the gypsy life may have worn off after fifteen years, but she loved Saul and clung to the marriage. As they were separating, my grandmother Goshkin came to New York to "talk some sense" into him. She failed. In Saul's play *The Wrecker*, written during these years, his protagonist uses a crowbar to demolish the apartment he and his wife shared. He explains to his mother-in-law that in order to go forward the past had to be destroyed.

Two decades later, Saul told Barley Alison, his English literary agent, "Reichian therapy broke up my first marriage."

In late 1951 Saul returned to Salzburg and Paris, probably to be with Nadine. In his absence, the rebellious eighteen-year-old daughter of a neighbor moved into our apartment to take care of me and to escape her mother. According to her, my mother had a brief affair with her hairdresser while Saul was away. The night of his return, Anita went to bed early, provocatively leaving him alone with the highly attractive sitter. Both told me they began to neck. Saul later said that he quickly realized it was crazy and stopped. The sitter reported that Anita came out of the bedroom, by the sitter's account to prevent her from revealing Anita's affair, though my view is that Anita was testing Saul and that he had failed. The young woman went home, and I can only imagine the argument that followed.

Saul told me about the impending end of the marriage on a bench in Central Park. I responded by making a snowball and letting fly at a nearby pigeon. What I really wished for was the courage to hit my father with the snowball. Under the childhood anger my father expected and hoped to see was sadness born of losing the parent who understood me best. At eight, I felt like a deep-sea diver cut off from my air supply.

Saul wrote *Augie March* during the lowest point in my parents' marriage. In the novel he describes Augie's trip to Mexico with a woman companion, Thea Fenchel, who invites him to help her to train an eagle to hunt giant iguanas. Contrary to its reputation as a wild animal, the great hunter dislikes the dangers of the chase and soon comes to prefer being tethered and hand-fed. In an echo of the near end of my parents' marriage in Mexico a

Lescha and her children, 1918. Left to right: Saul, Lescha, Morris (rear), Samuel, and Jane.

Anita Goshkin at sixteen.

Saul at sixteen.

Saul and Anita, 1937.

Ethel and Benjamin Freifeld. (Courtesy of Judith Freifeld Ward)

Sam Freifeld.

Herb and Cora Passin.

Saul with Oscar and Edith Tarcov.

Saul, Anita, and Harold "Kappy"
Kaplan, 1940.

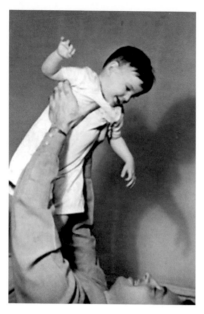

Saul and Greg, 1945.

Greg and Grandma Goshkin.

Isaac Rosenfeld and daughter, Nitza.

Oscar and Miriam Tarcov.

Herb, Mitzi, and Jane McClosky.
(Courtesy of Mitzi McClosky)

Arthur Herschel Lidov.

"Saul Bellow" by Arthur Lidov, ink on paper,
1947. (National Portrait Gallery, Smithsonian
Institution © Alexandra Lidov)

decade earlier, Augie, no doubt to prove to himself that he is unfettered, is all too easily seduced into helping another woman escape a failing romance. Augie returns from his mission of mercy to find that Thea has gone off on yet another adventure with a new male companion. She rejects the lonely Augie's belated proclamation of love and leaves him to fend for himself.

Just as Saul's literary character uses one woman to sever the ties that bind him to another, my father used an epidemic of philandering in Paris to escape what he considered Anita's control and to communicate that he wanted out. But Augie's ruminations about freedom's illusions reveal my father's deepest feelings about his marriage to my mother. Saul, like Augie, knew he had wronged Anita by going off with other women. In a harsh novelistic self-indictment, Saul cedes my mother the moral high ground, comparing his love, tainted by chronic sexual and personal selfishness, with her unselfish love. Saul's post-divorce "freedom" was to be short-lived. His romance with Alexandra Tschacbasov, who became Saul's second wife— a woman from a truly bohemian family and a damsel also in distress—was already deepening. It was Anita, the more independent of the two, who was to be free for a decade.

Chapter Five

HEARTACHE: 1952–56

S AUL'S DEPARTURE SPLIT my life in two. My father, in
many ways a kid who never grew up, who often worked at
home, and who understood my feelings, was no longer an everyday presence in my life. After six years of the gypsy life, I
had few friends from the neighborhood and was painfully shy.
I was lonely, sad, and now a latchkey kid in the Forest Hills
apartment living with a depressed mother. Every other weekend and for one summer month I had emotionally sustaining
visits with Saul that I tried desperately to prolong but that
ended in sadness at being away from the person who was essentially my best friend. Shuttling between two existences only
worsened my misery.

In Forest Hills I went off to school with a liverwurst sandwich
in my lunch box and came home to an empty house with a
snack in the fridge. After eating I would dress myself head to
toe in a cowboy outfit and head upstairs to our neighbors'
apartment to watch *The Lone Ranger* and *Hopalong Cassidy* while
I waited for Anita to come home. My mother was mortified
that I had so readily abandoned the European culture she and

Saul had tried to cultivate for American television. Anita was tending her own wounds and had less room than usual for my sadness. At dinner soon after the separation, I asked for kumquats for dessert. Anita said no. I complained that we used to have them when Saul was there and we were a family. She countered, "We're not a family anymore." I left the room, crushed.

Anita wrote a stoic letter to Sonia about the marriage ending but refused to grant Saul a divorce. The legal wrangling dragged on for years. Strapped for funds, Anita appealed to Grandpa Bellow for the money to buy a winter coat. She intended to make Saul look bad, but crying poverty did not endear her to the Bellows. Even after fifteen years of relying on her income, Saul wrote letters to friends and family during their legal battles about Anita wanting blood, making her out to be money hungry. The very idea of making regular payments, most of all alimony, infuriated him. When Saul dropped me off from custodial visits, it was rare that he left without taking a piece of fruit from the fridge, fruit for which he felt he was paying, and putting a few books under his arm. And he needled Anita. With one monthly check my father included a sarcastic note that read, "Hooray for socialism in one country!" His implication, clear to my mother, was that if Trotsky's notions for worldwide revolution had prevailed as they had both hoped, he would not have to send her alimony. Years later Anita told me that during their long, bitter financial battle, she had a recurrent fantasy that Saul was going to pick me up for custodial visits in a gold Cadillac. Despite the windfall provided by *Augie March,* he thought of himself as a starving artist who should not be burdened with mundane concerns like money. Beginning with his first successful novel, for decades Saul was never sure he had another novel within him that would sell, let alone sell well.

Anita avoided dating and even discouraged attention from men. But, given her great beauty, they were drawn to her. Lillian Blumberg, then living in Greenwich Village with the art critic Clement Greenberg, tried to maintain friendly relations with both Saul and Anita when they separated. In the spirit of women's equality, liberalism, and Reichianism, Lillian invited both to a party. A male guest flirted with my mother and, despite their separation, Saul got so upset that the two men got into a fight in the street over Anita.

When the final divorce papers were served, my usually stoic mother went into her bedroom, closed the door, and sobbed. Anita righted herself after several unhappy years. She went into therapy, developed a more positive self-image than she had during my parents' marriage, and completed her social work master's degree in 1957. She remained a strong proponent of personal and political freedom, liberation, idealism, tolerance, socialism, free speech, and birth control. On a visit with the McClosky family about two years after Saul moved out, a reinvigorated Anita confessed to Mitzi that she now repeated the same amusing stories Saul had told and retold in Minneapolis that had so irritated her. On that same visit Anita delivered a description of sexual intercourse and birth control methods to me, aged eleven, and Jane McClosky, one year my senior, so graphic that it became family lore.

During the school year Saul picked me up for bimonthly visits. Anticipating a few happy hours with my father, I'd watch for him out the front window as I waited. He was often late and sometimes did not show up at all. I do not remember either parent criticizing the other during those years, but decades later Anita told me how crushed I was when disappointed by my father not showing up. Going to meet Saul one day, Anita and I were on the subway but the train would not budge from the stop before ours. I panicked, fearful that he'd leave and not calmed by Anita's reassurances. Finally we got out of the subway and took a cab two blocks, where we found him.

On cold winter Saturday afternoons, Saul and I would go to MoMA, look at the pictures, eat looking out at the sculpture garden, and watch an old movie in the basement theater. Or we would go to the Met, where I enjoyed the armor. Another amusement was joining Sam Goldberg, Saul's lawyer and friend, during long hours in the used-book stores just north of the Village. Sam's love of books exceeded even my father's. Books spilled out of his dresser drawers and were piled high in every room of his two houses. The reward for my patience in the bookstores was lunch at the Eighth Street Delicatessen. My favorite outing was to attend a double or triple feature of W. C. Fields and Mae West or the Marx Brothers. Saul and I knew every quip by heart and laughed until our sides hurt. For years my father used humor to jolly me out of the bad mood that always overtook me when it was time to say goodbye.

Saul understood my black moods because he had so many of them himself, and because he felt responsible for my sadness. His life was moving very fast. Saul was never in the same place for long, worsening our visits because I was often in new places and with unfamiliar people, mostly adults. Our summer month was better because we established a daily routine and had plenty of time with each another. After one summer visit I remember as particularly happy, I returned to Forest Hills and Anita made my favorite dinner to celebrate. After she went to work the next morning, I found myself alone in the apartment. Lonely and upset, I called Saul, and he met me for lunch at the Met. His understanding of my sadness was comforting that afternoon but offered no real substitute for his daily presence in my life.

After the first miserable year with my parents apart, I hit upon the idea of a dog. Lobbying hard with both parents, I clinched the deal with the promise "If I got a dog, I'd never be sad again." Anita agreed after setting the condition that Saul house-train the dog. By then Saul's future second wife, Alexandra Tschacbasov, was joining us during some of my visits. Anita Phillips, a former roommate of Alexandra's, owned a dachshund about to have puppies, and she gave me one. My father named her Lizzie after Elizabeth Barrett Browning, because both had sad eyes. Saul and I trained Lizzie that summer and I took her with me on visits to him until I left for college.

Alexandra Tschacbasov, whom I always called Sasha, was an only child born in 1931. Her mother, Esther, was a gentle, kindhearted woman. By the time I met Esther she had left Sasha's father but lived a few blocks from him. After Saul and Sasha married, Esther joined us for weekends, entertaining me with card games during the interminable mornings when my father was writing and everyone else was supposed to remain quietly occupied.

Sasha describes her father as completely self-centered. Dissatisfied with his middle-class Chicago origins and the life of a businessman, he took the family to France when Sasha was one so he could study painting. For three years he studied with Fernand Léger and adopted the name Nahum Tschacbasov, which was similar to that of his original Russian family. They returned to New York and moved frequently between lofts and studios in Manhattan and Brooklyn. Sasha was a favorite subject, and Nahum's paintings of her as a little girl still adorn her walls.

Sasha was a tough little girl who once climbed to the top of a jungle gym where she threw rocks at bullies who had chased her. She attended local public schools until the age of eight, then went off to a boarding school about an hour outside of New York City. As a teenager Sasha was an athletic swimmer and a fearless diver. During her high school years, the family moved into the Chelsea Hotel. As Sasha grew to maturity, she accused her father of sexually abusing her. Sasha put an end to the abuse after about a year, but she never forgave him and remained so angry that she never allowed her son, my brother Adam, to meet his maternal grandfather.

At seventeen, Sasha left for college at Bennington. After graduation, she returned to New York and worked briefly at the *Partisan Review*, where she met Saul. During these years, she was taken with the mystery of the Catholic Church, took instruction with Bishop Fulton Sheen, and converted. After she left the *Partisan Review* Sasha worked as an editor on two Catholic magazines. Saul found Sasha's commitment to Catholicism an obstacle to sex. He determined that Ted Hoffman, a lapsed Catholic now living in New York, should go and "reason" with Sasha. He coached Ted to make the logical argument that Protestantism was based in "protest" against the strictness of the Catholic Church. Ted chuckled as he told me the story years later, musing on why he ever undertook such a fool's errand.

To lighten the burdens of child care on him and to provide playmates for me, Saul would attach himself to intact families with children. But I wanted to be with Saul and found these children poor substitutes. Monroe Engel, Saul's editor at the Viking Press, left publishing and went to Princeton for a Ph.D. The Engels and their children became a big part of our family life for several years. Sasha, by now in a serious relationship with Saul, became such a regular visitor in Princeton that for many years I thought the Engels had introduced her to Saul. With the help of Delmore Schwartz, my father found a temporary teaching position at Princeton. Delmore lived with his wife, Elizabeth Pollet, up a dirt road in rural New Jersey. Once again I was the only child surrounded by adults. Saul, Delmore, and Elizabeth took time out to toss a football around with me, but I entertained myself during their interminable conversations playing with Delmore's miniature pool table, a toy he eventually gave me.

Delmore was descending into madness, most likely bipolar disorder. His expansive ideas, full of charm and delivered with amazing conviction in an incessant flow of grandiose notions, predicted a cultural transformation of America during the administration of Adlai Stevenson he fully anticipated. He was convinced that democracy was about to deliver on its potential to change the world by spreading culture in a golden age to come—a notion that greatly appealed to my father. Delmore's already precarious mental state soon spiraled downward, landing him in Bellevue's psychiatric ward. He abused pills and alcohol and got progressively worse.

In Manhattan, Saul attached us to Pat and Dorothy Covici for holiday meals at their apartment. Pat, John Steinbeck's long-time editor, had taken over as Saul's editor at the Viking Press when Monroe left. According to my father, Steinbeck depended so heavily on Covici's editorial advice that the relationship took on a father-son dimension. Saul maintained that his author-editor relationship was not one of dependency, but my father's letters to Pat, including one addressed to "Father Covici," show how much my father also relied on him.

For several years we spent a month of summer on the far end of Long Island or on Cape Cod. During my weekend visits, Saul would take a day off from writing, but during the summer I was left to entertain myself every morning while Saul wrote. Swimming filled most afternoons, and there were frequent cocktail parties in the early evenings. Anticipating my boredom as the only child in attendance, Saul let me bring Lizzie to these parties. I set myself up on lawn furniture and fed the dog potato chips that went right through her. Before attending a party at Edmund Wilson's Wellfleet home, Saul appeared quite nervous. He told me our host was a famous literary critic and asked me to be on my best behavior. The weather must have kept us inside. When I fed Lizzie her quota of potato chips with the usual results, a mortified Saul had to clean the dog poop from Wilson's Oriental carpet.

Unable to divorce Anita in New York State, Saul went to Nevada in 1955. He lived at Pyramid Lake in a shack surrounded by tumbleweed and sent me a fragrant sprig that I kept by my bed and sniffed frequently during his long absence. He was soon joined by Sasha, whom he was anxious to marry. They went into Reno about once a week to shop and play blackjack at Harold's Club. Arthur Miller was near Reno, too, and also divorcing his first wife. Marilyn Monroe visited him there, and the two couples struck up a friendship.

Back in New York, the foursome made a date for dinner. Over a drink in the Millers' home, Arthur entertained Saul and Sasha while Marilyn was dressing. After an hour or more, Arthur excused himself. Soon he returned and urged Sasha to go into the bedroom and help Marilyn decide what to wear. Sasha quickly helped her choose something and the famished couples went out to Rocco's, a favorite restaurant of Saul's on the northern edge of Little Italy. Marilyn wore some sort of disguise, but word of her presence got out. Having recently thrown over Joe DiMaggio for Arthur, she was none too popular in the Italian community, and an unruly crowd formed on the street. Saul had to get his car and pull right in front of the restaurant so Marilyn could get into it without an ugly scene. For several years, Saul brought me greetings from Marilyn. When I was thirteen, I met her when he and Arthur were inducted into the National Academy of Arts and Letters. I remember her as very beautiful and surrounded by men, but she took a minute to say hello to me. Anita was upset that I met famous people though Saul. She felt left behind, and the gold Cadillac in which she imagined Saul was now full of celebrities.

I went with Anita to Chicago, where Grandma Goshkin and Grandpa Bellow both lived, but more often I went with Saul. He and I took the eighteen-hour train ride from New York on the Twentieth Century Limited. I drank ginger ale in the club car while we played casino—to me it was the height of luxury. If Saul and I drove, we'd pass the time singing "Old Hogan's Goat," "The Eddystone Light," "Anne Boleyn," and the songs Aunt Jenny had sung to Saul in Lachine during the First World War.

I most remember Fanny's sloppy kisses and Jewish dishes such as boiled tongue and stuffed cabbage. I was supposed to kiss Grandpa but found his face rough from intermittent shaving. Abraham was in the habit of distributing silver dollars to his grandchildren. I kept mine in a metal cigarette box acquired in France, along with a huge wad of czarist Russian rubles Saul had given me to play with. During a summer visit, I decided to water the flowers in Grandpa's backyard. I was wearing socks but no shoes and he anticipated that I'd make a muddy mess. I insisted that I could keep them dry and refused to take them off. Saul, still an indulgent parent then, stuck up for me. Grandpa was right. I did make a mess.

During Grandpa's last years, the entire Bellow family, including Saul when he was in town, would go over to Abraham and Aunt Fanny's for Sunday afternoon meals. The regular attendees were Morrie, his wife, Marge, and their children, Lynn and Joel; Sam, his wife, Nina, and their children, Lesha and Shael; and Jane, her husband, Charlie Kauffman, and their sons, Larry and Bobby. When Grandma Lescha's name came up, her children spoke of her with great reverence. The afternoons were largely harmonious until the conversation turned to money, which shattered the superficial the goodwill. While the parents visited, the kids played intensely competitive games of Monopoly.

Abraham found financial threats the best way to reassert his waning paternal authority. His frequent fights with his children often ended with his announcement that he was changing his

will and disinheriting the current offender. He would go so far
as to call his lawyer, often in the middle of the night, with in-
structions to draw up a new will excluding that child. Morrie
tired of this routine early on and turned his nose up at his share
to emphasize its paltry size, but Abraham's mercurial threats
had serious consequences for Sam, Jane, and Saul, whose fragile
finances made him particularly vulnerable. My father would
rush back to Chicago to learn about the new will. By the time
the family had assembled at Grandpa's insistence to hear of the
new asset division, he and the offending child had patched things
up and the crisis would blow over until Abraham pulled the
same stunt again and the whole scene was repeated.

My grandfather was often provocative, setting even his grandchildren against one another. On the night before my cousin
Joel's bar mitzvah, he and our cousin Shael stayed at Abraham
and Fanny's. Oblivious to Joel's nervousness before he was to
read from the Torah in public, Grandpa compared him unfavorably to Shael, whose family was more religious. The next morning at the synagogue, in a typical disruptive gesture, Abraham
took a public shot at Joel's father. Morrie had invited business
associates and political connections, Jews and non-Jews, on
whom he wanted to make a good impression. But when my
grandfather rose to speak after the reading, he asserted that if you
have a choice, you should "always do business with a Jew!"

When *The Adventures of Augie March* was published, my
grandfather took considerable pride in his rabbi's praise of the
book. Despite turning down my father's requests for money, he
continued to worry about Saul's financial prospects and told
Sam to watch out for the welfare of his kid brother.

In 1955, when he was seventy-eight, Grandpa had a fatal heart attack. Morrie used his connections to secure a police escort complete with sirens from the synagogue to the cemetery. Saul joked about the irony that Abraham, who was running from the police most of his life, was accompanied by them on his last journey. After the funeral Aunt Fanny confessed to Saul that Grandpa had wanted to have sex the evening before he died, but she put him off because he had the sniffles. Her story cemented my father's awe of Abraham as a tough, horny old bird. Despite their arguments, one of which included a threat by Abraham to come after Saul with a gun if he asked for money again, Saul grieved deeply. When Ruth Miller, a former student, came to pay a condolence call, she found my father weeping as he listened to Mozart's *Requiem*.

Seize the Day reflects Saul's lost hope of approval from his father. Abraham was not only unable to show Saul his love but also had formed a critical judgment of his youngest as an overgrown crybaby who had failed to absorb the lesson life taught him: the necessity for emotional toughness. I think that my father agreed but could do little to control his emotions. A film version of the novel was produced three decades later. The actor Joseph Wiseman, who played Dr. Adler, Tommy Wilhelm's father, bore an uncanny physical resemblance to Grandpa and perfectly captured his harshness toward his son. After having witnessed such scenes between my father and grandfather, I was riveted to the screen as Tommy begs his implacable father for money. I mentioned to several family members how struck I was by the film, and my words of praise got back to my father. Saul, who believed that writing was a far superior way to capture the essence of people than film, took offense. On our next visit, he complained about what he took to be my lack of appreciation of his novel and extended his criticism to my lack of interest in literature as a whole. I told him that I continued to read and love great writers of fiction, but that I could not appreciate his books as literature. "They're just too close," I said. As was his habit whenever, like it or not, he was confronted with an irrefutable position, he remained silent and never again brought up the subject.

Despite his threats Abraham did not disinherit any of his children, and Saul's share, about fifteen thousand dollars, was sufficient to buy a large house in the Hudson Valley. But Grandpa's threats had a salutary effect on Saul's behavior about money with his sons. Our father made it clear that each son was responsible for his own finances, thereby avoiding the destructive Bellow practice of mixing family and money matters.

After the death of their father, my uncles, aunt, and their families settled into midlife routines. Morrie was a wheeler-dealer in Chicago, and Marge ran their hotels day-to-day with a heavy but effective hand. Marge took great pride in her business acumen, and their relationship, half marriage and half business partnership, created a formidable team. Morrie, Marge, Lynn, and Joel lived in the penthouse of the Shoreland Hotel, which seemed palatial when I visited. As a teenager, Joel would use ten towels to dry off after a bath.

Freed from the constraints of watching over the Carroll Coal Company, Sam hit his stride as a businessman. He began a chain of profitable nursing homes and offered family members financial participation. I believe Sam hoped that spreading ample profits among the Bellows would promote the family concern and togetherness that he, too, prized from their days in Lachine. His wife, my aunt Nina, was a woman of ambition and energy, but in an era when having a working wife reflected poorly on a husband's ability to provide for his family, Sam forbade her to work outside the home. Nina, who came from a family of rabbis, prevailed at home. My cousins Lesha and Shael were raised in an observant Jewish household, and Sam rarely intervened.

Jane married Charlie Kauffman, a dentist who treated the Bellow family and, reportedly, possessed minimal technical skill. As a young husband, Charlie, bored by his marriage, led a double life. He went through the motions of domesticity but spent many hours gambling with shady characters. Jane was, by all accounts, a smothering mother to her children, Larry and Bobby. Anita derided Jane's germ phobias and her custom of boiling oranges before peeling them and wiping the rails of my cousins' crib with chemicals more harmful than any germ they might encounter licking them.

I did not live in Chicago after 1946 and had almost no relationships with my Bellow aunts, uncles, or cousins. I was used to the generosity of the doting Goshkins, all childless, who sent birthday presents and candy on Valentine's Day. My aunts Ida and Catherine stayed with us when they visited New York to attend the theater and Catherine offered to take me to any restaurant I named, although I always chose the Automat. I was hurt by the lack of attention I received from the Bellows and asked Anita why my rich uncle Morrie never sent me anything for my birthday.

Our years in the Hudson Valley anchored the only domestic life I had with my father after the divorce. Saul got a job teaching at Bard College and I summered on or near campus for years. At first he lived in a carriage house on the estate of Chanler Chapman, a wealthy local character who was related to the Astor family. Saul attended parties at the mansion house and must have been treated as a celebrity because he had to explain the word *lionize* to me when he used it to describe how he was treated there.

Ted and Lynn Hoffman, whom I already knew from Salzburg, lived on campus and often looked out for me. The Hoffman girls were too young to be of any interest, but I delighted in Ted's wit and infectious laugh. Curled up in a big chair in the Hoffman living room, I spent hours poring over the joke books Ted bought me. During Saul's second year at Bard, he shared the house with Ted during the week because Lynn had an editorial job at the Viking Press and stayed in Manhattan. Lynn told me that her presentation to the Viking marketing department about *The Adventures of Augie March* was interrupted by the delivery of an elegant package from California. John Steinbeck had sent his manuscript *East of Eden* in a hand-carved wooden box. It so impressed everyone that she could not turn their attention back to Saul's novel.

In fair weather we played volleyball or swam at the Bard pool. In foul we played basketball in the gym, where Sasha taught me to shoot the ball with one hand, since Saul knew only the old-fashioned two-handed set shot of his youth. Keith Botsford, a flamboyant character who attached himself to Saul for decades, lived on campus with his then wife, Ann. Saul, always in search of child care and entertainment for me, hit on the fine idea that Keith should give me tennis lessons. I believe Keith's father had played tennis on the Olympic team, and he was an excellent player. "Tennis lessons" consisted of his hitting shots difficult even for a skilled adult to return and me running after tennis balls. One of the most transparently competitive people I ever encountered, Keith could not stand to lose. Even in a game of Scrabble at the Hoffmans', he used the word *nuncio*, but substituted a *t* for the *c*. When challenged by Lynn, he went wild, claiming that it was an alternate spelling and refusing to admit defeat even when the dictionary failed to back him up.

Jack Ludwig was another flamboyant Bard character. He had a deep basso voice and sang in a college choral group that included Sasha. I don't know when Sasha and Jack's affair began, but by 1956 it was common for Saul, Sasha, and me, in some combination, to see Jack and his family almost daily. I spent endless adolescent hours in a nearby tree. In that favorite niche I was able to avoid both the boring adult conversation and having to play with Jack's daughter Susie, who was five years my junior, though, no doubt, bored as well.

Saul jokingly called the house he bought with his inheritance "Bellowview." Several miles from Bard, it was in a town called Tivoli. Just before we moved in, the Lane brothers, antique dealers who owned the house, held an auction I attended with Saul and his constant companion Jack. Included in the sale were the house's huge window screens; Saul was furious at having to pay for something he thought he already owned. He was convinced that the Lane brothers had removed valuable chandeliers too as well.

The house was huge. Half of the first floor was taken up by an elegant ballroom longer than a bowling alley, its fourteen-foot ceilings replete with ornate plaster foliage. The cost of heating the ballroom was beyond Saul, but the African violets that

Ralph Ellison, who visited often and later lived in the house, cultivated in its cool air flourished, even if we did not. Across the hall were the living room and Saul's study. Four large bedrooms, also with high ceilings, made up the next floor. You could see the Hudson River from the second-floor windows when the leaves had fallen. Above that was another floor, with smaller rooms once used to house servants but which was now sealed off also to prevent losing heat. Across from our front lawn, Chanler Chapman grew feed corn for his cows in a large field, and Saul often walked the narrow path around its perimeter alone or with adult friends. Behind the house there was a large overgrown garden where he and I picked our dessert from the raspberry bushes that grew half-wild on its edges.

For months we cooked and ate in an upper room because the basement, where the kitchen was planned, had no viable plumbing. Saul hired a contractor that fall but found that the interminable hammering interfered with his writing. He took off for the quiet of Yaddo, a writers' colony a few hours away, leaving Sasha to manage the contracting, which greatly irritated her and set the stage for disaster.

One morning in the summer of 1956 a phone call woke us with news that Isaac Rosenfeld had died in Chicago. Saul was inconsolable. Although I had only scattered memories of Isaac, I was saddened as well. According to his daughter Miriam, Oscar Tarcov lay on the couch all day immobilized in shock after he got the news. Saul could not make himself go to Isaac's funeral. Vasiliki, his widow, was furious with him, but my father was unable to see beyond his own grief.

Yet death, spiritual maladies, and suffering pervade *Henderson the Rain King*, written soon after Isaac and Grandpa died. Chan-

ler Chapman, a huge physical specimen who had correspond-
ingly large appetites and a disdain for convention, served as the
model for Eugene Henderson, Saul's tragicomic title character.
Saul included Chanler's nihilistic habit of breaking bottles with
his slingshot on a beach in Miami, leaving it covered with dangerous shards of glass. That oft-repeated story was a source of
family amusement, but many years later Chanler's nephew
(who became a friend of mine in California) told me his uncle
was hurt by Saul's novelistic exaggeration of his eccentricities.

In *Henderson the Rain King*, Gene Henderson chooses a life
path that brings him into contact with suffering and death. He
is haunted by the biblical line "a man of sorrow and acquainted
with grief," a phrase embedded in my memory after listening
to Handel's *Messiah* over and over on Saul's hi-fi. Born to material ease, Henderson's deepest desire is to be helpful. A zealous
blunderer who cannot contain his impulse to improve the lives
of others, he brings only more trouble to his intended benefi-
ciaries. The scorn he heaps on himself when he fails merely fans
his desire to be even more helpful. In the middle of Africa,
Gene meets a soul mate, King Dafu, a highly educated man to
whom he confides his dreams and fears. Dafu is on a quest to
find his deepest nature by calmly approaching a lioness who has
been captured and kept in a cave but is allowed to move unfettered in an attempt to commune with the spirit of an animal
that can kill him at any moment. Inspired by his friend's courage and eager to capture the beast's powers with his own soul,
Henderson agrees to follow along. Neither falls prey to the wild
beast, but Dafu is done in by lethal human ambition.

I believe the rapport between the literary characters Gene
Henderson and Dafu touches on my father's deep connection

with Isaac Rosenfeld. First in the books they read and later in
the larger scale of their own lives, these soul mates searched in
ideas and in experience for the deepest essences of humanity.
After Isaac's death, Saul compared himself unfavorably with
his friend, who was willing to take risks my hesitant and more
skeptical father was not. Isaac fully embraced life, including
Wilhelm Reich's emphasis on the body and on powerful emotion. Isaac showed courage that bordered on recklessness, for
which Saul believed he paid the ultimate price of an early
death. As opposed to *Seize the Day*, where Saul caricatured
Reichianism, *Henderson the Rain King* expresses my father's respect for Reich's emphasis on emotion as an unadulterated expression of what is essentially human, an emphasis that Saul's
rational side could never fully accept.

Chapter Six

BETRAYAL: 1957–62

SASHA SAID THAT when she became pregnant with Adam, Saul told her that raising one child was enough for him, pretty much disavowing the responsibilities of parenthood. However, I remember walking up hills with them to prepare her for childbirth, conversations about the baby's arrival, and going to see Adam in the hospital with an excited Saul. I recall Sasha at Tivoli when Adam was an infant. But by that summer Sasha and Adam were nowhere to be seen. My father, in a deadpan tone of voice, announced that she was moving to Brooklyn to "get away and think." Meanwhile Jack Ludwig was driving down to Brooklyn on a regular basis, ostensibly to "mediate" between Saul and Sasha.

The kitchen was finished and Jesse Reichek, our friend from Paris, joined us while his wife, Laura, visited her family in France. Jesse drew and Saul wrote all morning, but by then I had a rickety bicycle to get me to the local swimming pool. The three of us christened the new kitchen by making potato pancakes and several batches of jam from our raspberry bushes, which turned every surface red. After dinner we played poker for matchsticks at our new dining room table. Our neighbors owned a dachshund that we mated with Lizzie. During the act, a loud noise frightened the dogs, who could not uncouple even with human help. It was quite a scene as Saul and Jesse tried to put an ice pack where the yelping dogs were joined. Jesse was with us, as he reminded me years later, when I was talking to Saul about an interest in the stock market, which I developed at thirteen with a friend from forest Hills. Apparently Saul was so distressed about the affinity I expressed for capitalism that it brought him to tears.

Eventually Sasha moved back to Tivoli, where she and I drew closer in rural isolation. Desperate for any distraction, I tagged along when she took Adam to Red Hook to grocery shop. By that time I had taken to bringing friends from Forest Hills with me for weekend visits, prompting Saul to complain, accurately, that I was putting barriers between us. One lad, Michael Riff, hit it off so well with my father that Michael confided his adolescent confusion about religion to Saul. Michael's father, a former communist and a nonpracticing Jew, sent him to an Orthodox Hebrew school to prepare for his bar mitzvah. The school insisted that Michael wear phylacteries, a cloth with fringes, commonly called *tsitsis*, worn under one's shirt. He confessed to Saul that he'd come home after studying Hebrew only to find that his mother had left him a snack of ham, a food forbidden to Jews. After carefully taking off his shirt before eating, Michael was concerned about getting nonkosher grease on his *tsitsis*. My father found Michael's dilemma amusing, and over the years he and I joked about it so often that the story became part of family lore.

Another visitor at Tivoli was my aunt Jane's son Larry, who spent several days there during one of my summer stays. According to our cousin Lynn, Larry idealized his uncle Morrie (Lynn's father). Morrie, always one to impress, encouraged his slavish admiration by lavishing money on Larry, further encouraging his sycophancy. During Larry's visit, money started to disappear from several purses. No doubt hoping to dispel his worst fears about his nephew, my father asked if I knew about the missing money. Outraged, I took him to my room, where my allowance for the last few weeks, except what I had spent on stamps for my collection, was spread out on the mantelpiece. "That's all the money I have," I yelled, pointing to several dollars and a handful of change. Saul left my room in a silence that typified his response to being outflanked. In the arguments that were to come between us I came to understand his rare lack of words as acquiescence without having to admit defeat.

The money continued to disappear. Apparently, cash left out in the open did not appeal to Larry's kleptomania, which turned out to be just the tip of the iceberg. Larry joined the army, got into trouble for stealing and perhaps more, and ended up in the military prison at the San Francisco Presidio. The night before he was scheduled to be released, he was found hanged in his cell. The events that surrounded his death were vague, so our uncle Sam went to San Francisco to try to get to the bottom of a matter that grew more sordid with every detail he was able to uncover. Sam stopped asking questions, but the whole family was devastated by Larry's suspicious death.

Life with Anita continued in Forest Hills and I began to settle in. After my years at the Queens School, in the fall of 1955, I returned to P.S. 175, which was right down the street, for the fifth grade. For the first time in my life I started to make friends with classmates who lived nearby. Academically, a traditional elementary school was a rude awakening, as I lacked several skills, including writing in longhand. I was so far behind that my teacher hinted to Anita at their parent-teacher conference that I might be a bit "slow." Despite her concerns, the next year I passed a test that allowed me to do three years of junior high school in two. Unfortunately, my lack of academic discipline caught up with me again and I had to return to regularly paced classes. It was around this time, when Saul brought me home after a custodial visit, that my permissive parents sat me down and simply asked me whether or not I wanted to have a bar mitzvah. Since my new friends all complained about the Hebrew lessons they had to attend after school, I said no, and they accepted my decision as final.

During the mid-1950s, my New York family consisted of Anita, me, and Anita's cousin Beebee, who was by then married to Francis de Regniers. Francis was a stuffy Frenchman she had met working in an Egyptian refugee camp after World War II, and Beebee had invented an entirely new identity for him that included a last name "borrowed" from a blue-blooded French family. Suspicious of the whole story, her parents had asked Saul to investigate his background when we were living in Paris. It turned out Francis was an accountant named Gahlager, and Saul used Beebee's invention of an aristocratic identity for him as a primary example of her excessive romanticism.

Beebee did not have children, but, as her careers as an editor and author of marvelous children's books illustrate, she was always a child at heart. She doted on me. She read books to me in utero and spoiled me with attention and birthday gifts carefully picked every year to reflect my current interest. I repaid

Beginning in my adolescence, when the two of us were alone, my father would inquire after what he termed my inner life. Initially I was a bit confused, but soon realized he was asking me to consider whether or not I was content with myself. This began a regular dialogue we came to call "real conversations." At first they were dominated by Saul's recurrent explanations about why he had left Anita, including her rigidity, the envelope in her dresser with his name on it, and even her boring recipe for a tasteless tuna casserole, a dinner staple that we both disliked. The content expanded over decades to include family, our sociopolitical differences, and eventually our shared past; they remained a significant feature of our time together.

Saul and Sasha kept me insulated from their marital battles, and he refrained from telling me the details of her affair with Jack for several more years. I witnessed a great deal from the sidelines, and my later reading of *Herzog* provided an additional perspective on what I remember and was offered by Saul and Sasha by way of explanation.

When it came to the affair between Sasha and Jack Ludwig, my father kept his head in the sand for an astronomically long time. He accepted Sasha's explanations, rationalized Jack's visits to Brooklyn, and was convinced of their loyalty, partly because he basked in Jack's fawning. By thirteen I had begun to argue with Saul. During a conflict one summer that lasted a few days, Jack offered to be my confidant, "in case you needed someone to talk to." I spurned his overture; something about his tone gave me the creeps. I'd venture that Jack was trying to enlist my trust like he had my father's, by being my "pal."

In my teens I had been too young to recognize Jack's

her by getting Beebee into the petting zoo in Central I
which she loved but which adults could not enter witho
accompanying child under twelve.

Beebee, Francis, Anita, and I celebrated Thanksgivir
my birthday with elegant dinners that were often follow
play or skit Beebee orchestrated. When the Tarcovs m
New York in the late 1950s, they became part of our f
had become a huge baseball fan, and on their first vis
apartment I kept showing Oscar items of interest in a l
of baseball statistics. Oscar must have recognized that
for a day-to-day father was behind my attempt to m
his attention. The Tarcovs joined us for holiday c
and Oscar often ended these family parties with h
joy, a few expressive steps that ended with his long fr
on the nearest couch. No other man I knew openl
warmth. Oscar's love for his children and his wife
ble, and there was room in his heart left over for n

My father's heart was also full of such warmth,
not express it as freely as Oscar. And yet, early
sensed that my father understood my emotions
Anita did not. My first direct hint of the impor
sentiments to me, to Saul, and between us ca
sixteen. I bought Saul a humorous Father's Day
"To Me Fodder." It was unusual for me to t
Mother's or Father's Days, because both parents
capitalist excuses to buy greeting cards. I ov
hesitation because the interior of the card re
like a mudder to me, fodder," a line that co
truth about the emotional differences betwe
as parents.

chronic fawning over my father. Ten years ago I met Joseph Frank, the biographer of Dostoyevsky, and his wife, who were at the University of Minnesota when Saul, Sasha, Jack, and Laya Ludwig left Bard for Minneapolis. Both Franks went out of their way to decry the extremity of Jack's sycophantic behavior. As deferential as he may have been to Saul and to the Franks, he was pompous and full of himself with Bard undergraduates. Ted Hoffman described walking across campus with Jack while he loudly dispensed unsolicited advice on the best kind of condoms to incredulous students passing by. Jack accompanied Ted and Lynn Hoffman to Poughkeepsie when she went into labor. Ted thought he ought to stay at the hospital, but Jack, who claimed to "know all about these things," told him the labor was going to take hours and took Ted out for a beer. Ted returned to the hospital in the nick of time, almost missing the birth of his first child.

After several separations and what must have been horrific arguments, Saul hoped the already rocky marriage might get a new start in Minneapolis, where he had been offered a teaching appointment for the academic year 1958–59. Saul was once again relegated to Minnesota's humanities department, but after the publication of *Augie March* he was able to insist on a teaching appointment for Jack. Still blinded by misplaced trust, Saul shipped Sasha and Adam off to Minneapolis to find an apartment. Soon Jack showed up, and he and Sasha went off "apartment hunting" for days while Mitzi McClosky took care of Adam.

Saul mistrusted therapy after his Reichian analysis, but in Minneapolis he agreed when Sasha demanded that he try it again, no doubt a sign of his desperation to preserve their marriage. A

decade earlier when we had lived in Minneapolis, Herb Mc-
Closky had urged Saul to meet Dr. Paul Meehl, a brilliant academic psychologist who collaborated with Herb's research in
political science. Saul had been favorably impressed by his intelligence and, in the interim, Dr. Meehl had secured some clinical
training. Saul now sought him out as a therapist.

After more than six months of individual analysis with Saul,
Dr. Meehl took on Sasha as a patient as well. His dismissive attitude toward clinical boundaries, which included kissing Sasha
in front of Saul during a party at the McCloskys', underscored
his arrogant failure to refer Sasha to a colleague as soon as he
learned she was having an affair with Saul's best friend. Not surprisingly, Saul became less interested in self-examination than
in pressing Dr. Meehl for information about what Sasha was
up to.

Dr. Meehl was yet another expert Saul brought in when
practical matters, in this instance a deteriorating marriage, were
too complex to be ignored. Rather than investigating their
competency, Saul chose advisers on the basis of personal trust
and expediency. In exchange, Saul expected loyalty and quick
results, no matter how difficult the task. Dr. Meehl delivered
neither, but failure never stopped Saul from soliciting more advice. For years he continued to laud successive reality instructors
who arrived full of optimism and were all too happy to shower
my desperate father with even more conflicting and often non-
sensical advice.

My father's novels are full of well-meaning friends, lawyers,
schemers, and advisers brimming with helpful solutions for a
series of narrators. Like Saul, his narrators usually ignore the advice and follow their own misguided instincts, which draw them

into a destructive vortex. In life, as in his novels, Saul's failed advisers were foils for his contradictory impulses and became the perfect scapegoats to shoulder most of the blame for the disasters that ensued. Many years later, as Saul was in the process of firing his umpteenth set of lawyers and accountants, my father confided that he never really gave practical matters any consistent attention and deserved the treatment he got.

Moses Herzog is my father's prototypical example of a trusting man surrounded by an army of betrayers, figurative and literal. The figurative betrayers are men, great and small, whose abstract advice fails to be of sufficient help to a desperate man. Hoping for more clarity in one instance, Moses chides the philosopher Nietzsche's discussion of the quotidian—an overly abstract concept that offers little comfort to a man merely trying to live through yet another day filled with suffering. The literal betrayers are Madeleine Herzog, a wife who repays Moses's protective sentiments by sleeping with his best friend; Valentine Gersbach, his erstwhile confidant, to whom Moses pours out his heart while Valentine is sleeping with Madeleine; and Dr. Edvig, the cerebral psychiatrist who appears blind to both Madeleine's guile and how important his therapist's allegiance had become to a desperate Moses.

Sasha maintained that the true passion of the affair was between Saul and Jack. She underlined her point by calling Jack *Saul's* valentine, not hers. Near *Herzog's* conclusion, Moses accuses Valentine of seeking him through Madeleine's flesh. Regardless of Jack's intentions toward Saul, Sasha's willingness to persist in the affair had much to do with her anger about the vivid details of Saul's own affairs that my father (perhaps bragging) told Jack about and that Jack relayed to Sasha. Were that not enough, Saul had dumped the tasks of the Tivoli kitchen remodeling on Sasha and disavowed a second parenthood.

Sasha was not motivated solely by retaliation, as the affair continued long after her marriage to my father ended. Sasha and Adam moved to Great Neck, where Jack had a nearby teaching appointment. Five years later, Sasha and I had a nasty fight about Jack, during which I criticized and she defended the continuing affair. A decade later, Adam, then sixteen, asked me why I thought his parents' marriage did not work out. I answered that both of his parents were so intensely in love that neither knew how to handle their passions.

Saul was attracted to Sasha's beauty, wit, and charm. A bohemian past made her a better candidate to continue the freewheeling gypsy life that Anita would not. But Sasha, a young woman who had escaped from an abusive father and was a brief convert to Catholicism, was a damsel in distress I believe Saul sought to rescue. There is a poem my father recited to me as a child that recurs throughout *Herzog* and, I believe, sheds light on his expectation of trust from Sasha: *I love little pussy her coat is so warm, and I'll sit by the fire and give her some food, and pussy will love me because I am good.* The helpless little creature in the poem is supposed to love you, to be grateful to you, and to return your affections if simply kept warm and fed. Saul expected loyalty in return for his protective love. But the last phrase of the poem reveals that Saul understood the selfish side of his love. Despite how well they are treated, kitties grow into independent cats, and damsels who appear to be in distress may actually have strong wills. After he "rescued" Sasha, Saul counted on her gratitude to keep her loyal, while he continued to do as he wished. Sasha did not share Saul's agenda, and gave him a heaping tablespoon of his own philandering medicine.

In my view, Saul's connection to Jack resided in the man's tolerance for suffering, his capacity to absorb feelings, and his ability to appear sympathetic to Saul's constant complaining. Jack suffered palpably every day. One leg was far shorter than the other, and he walked with a pronounced limp. Worse, he suffered from a joint disease that flared up painfully and forced him to remain in bed until it subsided. Jack's palpable suffering in silence made a deep impression on my father. Perhaps it reminded him of Abraham's stoicism in Lachine, which he contrasted unfavorably with his own chronic complaining. No matter the reason, Saul's trust in Jack remained unshaken for years, likely because my father could not let himself suspect disloyalty or deception from a fellow deep sufferer.

In the pages of *Herzog*, Moses Herzog is attracted to Valentine Gersbach's "great heart," which is so big that it "could absorb an ocean of feelings." Moses attributes that heart to a terrible accident that Valentine suffered in childhood. The suffering Valentine endured while he continued to absorb Moses's pain stands in direct contrast to Dr. Edvig's cold, clinical manner. After a disappointing therapy session that makes him feel *worse*, Moses immediately turns to Valentine for the solace he so desperately needs. In one of his letters Moses castigates Dr. Edvig, ending with the line "I was your patient . . ." It is a protest and a plea that reveals Saul's genuine desire for help and his expectation of loyalty from a psychiatrist Saul thought Sasha was able to wrap around her little finger.

I have wondered why Saul was so blind to such blatant

deception. The answers lie in his facility with logic, his inclination to trust, and his inability to see guile in others that his hardheaded older brothers would never have missed. My father could and did argue either side of a question with equal vigor and conviction. He used or misused logic to compartmentalize his life, to behave as he wished without palpable guilt, and to deceive. He was thus able to convince himself of facts not in evidence, in this instance that Jack and Sasha were trustworthy.

When Saul finally wised up, he was like a wounded animal. He bad-mouthed Sasha and Jack to anyone who would listen. On a visit to Vasiliki Rosenfeld's not long after he realized what was going on, I could hear him ranting through the closed door. In my favorite Chinese restaurant in 1960, he began to complain to me about her. Sixteen years old and fond of Sasha, I stuck up for her. In my own defense as much as Sasha's, I claimed that Anita's experience as a social worker had taught me something about understanding people, and that knowledge assured me that Sasha was a good person. It was a ridiculous argument Saul pretty much demolished. But I was not deterred and kept up my relationship with Sasha for the rest of her life.

Herzog describes a man, Moses, clawing his way back to sanity after a terrible betrayal by two people he dearly loved has sorely taxed his grasp on what is real. Saul's protagonist rights himself much as my father must have. After the infidelity, Moses engages in a highly erotic affair that reaffirms his sexual desirability and, after a mishap, finds reassurance in belonging to a protective family. A highly agitated Moses gets into a car accident during a custodial visit with his young daughter, and is pulled over by the Chicago police. Instead of keeping his wits, he takes flight into a set of abstract, speculative ideas, which is exactly what my father did when he was overwhelmed by real events. But Moses Herzog cannot find sufficient solace in mere ideas, and I am convinced Saul was never sufficiently comforted by them either.

It is not until Moses is enveloped in the warm, protective care of his brother that he can calm down and regain his bearings. Most important, after having his trust betrayed, Moses retreats to fond memories of scene after scene from his childhood and finally pens a letter of gratitude to his mother in the great beyond. Like his narrator, my father found the solace he so desperately needed in his Rock of Gibraltar during troubled times, the reassuring memories of Grandma Lescha's great heart.

While Saul and Sasha battled, the advent of puberty and high school did me a world of good. I developed an active social life, which included hours playing schoolyard basketball, going to dances, and dating. I went to Manhattan on the subway, dropping in on Vasiliki Rosenfeld because girls from Forest Hills were very impressed that I actually knew someone who lived in the Village. Anita was happy to see me out and about after school and on weekends, and she supported my independence by insisting that I learn the full range of domestic skills, so I could take care of myself when I moved out.

My childhood sadness turned to adolescent anger. Arguments with both parents were open, direct, fierce, and usually grounded in my highly moralistic sense of right and wrong. My mother always took pride in how well she tolerated my anger, but when I exasperated her, she would say, "I can't wait until you grow out of this stage." I grew to hate that remark for trivializing something I felt strongly, and would sarcastically urge her to go back to her books on child rearing if she didn't know what to do with me. My father loved my retort, since Anita's formulaic child-rearing techniques confirmed the rigidity of her views that he often cited as his reason for leaving us.

For years Saul told me that he had found an angry teenager much easier to deal with than a morose child. No doubt he was relieved to see me put the sadness caused by his departure behind me. In later years, when I had established myself as a child therapist, Saul commented that I had turned the misery of my childhood into a career. I'd characterize my gift as being able to relate to boys who suffered broken hearts.

But Saul was sensitive to my criticism when directed at him. After discovering that he had not paid Anita's alimony for several months, I turned my moral indignation on him in a scathing letter. Anita, who had fought with Saul over money, knew I was putting my head in the lion's mouth and advised me to temper my outrage. Rather than telling me that his finances were none of my business, Saul sent me a letter justifying his behavior. He asked me to be fair to both parents. But he also accused me, now an avowed socialist, of being inconsistent and played on his status as a writer who cared little about money. There's a wonderful line about blood, rather than dimes, running through his veins. Fifty years later, what most surprises me most is how I took his response in stride. Doubtless I was already subscribing to his self-justification: that his career as an artist entitled him to let people down with impunity.

By the early 1960s Anita took a medical social work position at HIP, a prepaid group medical plan. For her, it was as
good as the socialized medicine she had dreamed of for decades.
I was at school and Anita was at work all week, but we usually
spent a few hours together Sunday morning reading the *New
York Times*. After years of avoiding men, Anita dated a widower
with three children who lived in Westchester County, just north
of Manhattan, for a year and we spent some weekends there.
She and I drove back to Forest Hills on Sunday nights, laughing
aloud at Jean Shepherd's funny, nostalgic monologues on the
car radio.

On Thanksgiving weekend 1961, Shirley Camper, an old
friend of Anita's who had spent many years in Madison, Wisconsin, invited her to a party. Her goal was to introduce Anita
to Basil Busacca, a recent widower Shirley knew from Madison
who was now teaching comparative literature at Occidental
College in Los Angeles. Anita and Basil hit it off immediately.
Less than a month later, at Christmas, my mother went to California to meet Basil's college-aged children while I visited Saul
in Tivoli.

As I began my last semester of high school, I remember
drifting off to sleep to the sound of Anita banging away on her
typewriter, writing long letters to Basil while chain-smoking.
Meanwhile, across the country, Basil was banging away on *his*
typewriter and then going out at midnight to post letters to
Anita. By March 1962, only four months after they had met,
they decided to marry. At my request Anita held off the wedding
until June; I did not want to change high schools for the final
three months of my senior year.

Basil planned to spend the summer in Forest Hills and

teach a course at Queens College. In September he and Anita would move to his house in South Pasadena, California, and I would go off to college. Their plan, while practical, was a disaster. Basil tried to impose his will on me, and I fought him at every turn. All that summer Anita was trapped between us as Basil and I battled. Saul tried to mollify me by predicting that I'd be grateful one day that Basil was there to protect and care for Anita. That would eventually prove true, but not during the hellish summer that marked the end of my childhood.

I met Susan Glassman, who would become my father's third wife, during my last years of high school. Susan was teaching English at the Dalton School, a private school in Manhattan, and had a small apartment in the city. She began to join us in Tivoli, and I always enjoyed her energy and engaging personality. Susan stopped teaching at Dalton but not before introducing me to a student named Lucy Saroyan, daughter of the author William Saroyan. I soon had a crush on Lucy and tried to dazzle her with my wit during long phone calls, but her interest in me faded after a few dates.

Susan was the only daughter of a successful orthopedic surgeon named Frank and a beautiful, stylish mother named Delores. Susan and her younger brother, Philip, grew up in material comfort. She graduated from a public high school and then from Wellesley College. Her father did not want her to go to graduate school, but Susan used her graduation gift to fund a master's program. I do not know how she met Philip Roth, whom she dated in the mid-fifties, but on one of their dates they went to a reading Saul gave at the University of Chicago, where she introduced herself to my father. Several years later, Susan was living in New York and seeing Saul romantically; she visited him while he was teaching in Puerto Rico. After their wedding in 1961, they spent an academic winter quarter at the University of Chicago, which was a prelude to leaving New York for Chicago and a permanent appointment for Saul on the university's Committee for Social Thought. He began in September 1962, the same month I began as a freshman at the College of the University of Chicago.

In the decade after we returned from Europe, Saul lost his father and his dear friend Isaac Rosenfeld. He failed in two marriages and had a son from both. Death, divorce, and betrayal shattered many of Saul's youthful hopes and naive illusions about how the world and human relationships were supposed to work. Apparently blessed with more lives than a cat, my father bounced back. What remains unclear is the extent to which he blamed himself for the marital failures and personal misery during that ten-year span and, perhaps more important, whether Saul's inner life had been affected by all the heartache he poured into the four novels that he produced: *The Adventures of Augie March*, *Seize the Day*, *Henderson the Rain King*, and *Herzog*.

GROWING APART

Chapter Seven

FAME AND MISFORTUNE: 1963–76

A RECEPTION FOR FRESHMEN foreshadowed changes to come. The event included a receiving line of university officials, to whom I introduced myself as Gregory Bellow. By the third handshake, they were calling me "Saul's son." Though Saul had just been appointed to the faculty, I chafed at his eminence on campus, and immediately it became clear to me that I could not stay in Chicago after my education and fully be my own person. Little did I suspect that, during the next dozen years, his fame would mushroom well beyond Chicago.

The undergraduate education I so wished for was a rude awakening. Everyone in the College was bright, and many were brilliant. For the first time in my life, I was trying as hard as I could but getting poor results that made me feel stupid. I became a frequent guest at Susan and Saul's modest two-bedroom apartment on Fifty-fifth Street during my freshman year. I sought their help with my papers, and her cooking was a decided improvement over dorm food. Susan's charm and wit were substantial, and we had many lively conversations. When I decided to major in psychology two years later, we had spirited but amicable disagreements about psychoanalytic schools of thought. However, I rarely made a visit there without having to perform a time-consuming physical chore for Susan, which I came to resent. Saul and I had a terrible argument in front of my dorm at the end of my freshman year when he broke a promise to take my suitcase to New York because Susan had filled the car with her own belongings.

During that year I had an up-and-down relationship with Saul. He was sympathetic about my academic struggles and my bitter arguments with my mother. Anita had reneged on her earlier commitment to pay half of my college expenses after she and Basil went through my education fund settling into their new life. Saul was supportive of her new marriage and assumed Anita's portion of my expenses. But he also decided that our physical proximity would afford him an opportunity to make up for past absences. At eighteen, the last thing I wanted was to get closer to my father, but Saul refused to take no for an answer. I enlisted the help of Ted Hoffman, who was passing through town. Somehow, over a drink, Ted got through to Saul, who backed off from a son who was now a young man.

We all knew Oscar Tarcov's heart was weak, but his death during my sophomore year and the events that surrounded his funeral dealt a serious blow to my trust in Saul. We all loved Oscar and I felt it imperative that Saul, Anita, or I attend the funeral. As the plans took shape I offered to go if Saul could not because Susan was pregnant. Saul assured me he'd go, but Susan began to have medical problems and he could not leave her. Thoughtlessly, he only told me after the funeral that he had not attended. I was livid that he hadn't called me in time to go in his place.

Oscar's death upset me deeply and aggravated my academic

struggles. By the middle of my sophomore year, I became quite depressed that I was trying so hard yet achieving such poor results. By then Anita and I had mended fences after a huge air-clearing fight with Basil that had been brewing since the tension-filled summer of 1962. I spoke with Saul and Anita about my frustrations, and we agreed I should go into therapy.

My psychiatrist followed the contemporary therapeutic custom of sitting in silence. I expected more direct help. His lack of participation strengthened my already fierce independence but only made it harder for me to appreciate the importance of other people. His occasional comments about my disinclination to say anything about our relationship fell on particularly deaf ears. Irritated by his lack of help, I had few insights in his office. Despite my resistance to him, I learned a great deal about myself thinking about our sessions when I was alone. As my therapy drew to a close, I said something in passing about Anita. My psychiatrist noted that my mother had been conspicuous in her absence from our sessions. It was then that I began a serious discussion of the way I protected myself by refusing to admit that I was affected by anyone—my mother, my father, my girlfriend, or him. I began to understand how my pessimism about permanent relationships with women was shaped by Saul's failed marriages and the ensuing enmity I witnessed. As the therapy progressed, I stopped fighting with my father and my current girlfriend. My academic problems faded after I became passionate about psychology.

During the Indian summer of 1964, my twentieth year, my father became Saul Bellow the famous author. *Herzog* was published, and his play *The Last Analysis* was produced on Broadway.

In late August I joined Saul, Susan, and my infant brother Daniel in New York. One sunny morning, Saul and I were walking down Fifth Avenue, having been instructed by Susan to buy me a "proper" suit for the upcoming festivities. We passed several bookstores, their enormous front windows filled with blue-jacketed copies of *Herzog*. Though we tried to ignore them, Saul and I finally stopped to gaze at one of the displays. He shrugged his shoulders, seemingly resigned to the changes that such public exposure was going to bring. For better or worse his life, as well as mine, was changed forever in those celebratory weeks. I chafed in my new wool suit and the loss of anonymity it represented. Susan, however, was in her element. Outgoing and dressed to kill for every event, she found living in the public eye in New York to be precisely how she had envisioned being married to Saul Bellow.

I watched rehearsals of *The Last Analysis* from the back rows of the dark Belasco Theater. Bummidge, the play's main character, is a self-styled philosopher-king who has an ambitious scheme to bring about an explosion of high culture in America by psychoanalyzing the masses over the radio. With a weak cast, the play was already foundering in rehearsal when Saul called in Ted Hoffman, who was then teaching drama in Pittsburgh. My father hoped Ted could help him negotiate the move from the familiar format of the novel to the unfamiliar stage. On opening night, I went to Sardi's with the cast to await reviews. Saul hoped for a critical success and was mindful of the money that comes with a hit Broadway play: six thousand dollars for Saul every week the play ran. But the reviews were harsh, and the play closed after two weeks.

The New York festivities for the novel and play were over by

October, and Saul, Susan, and I returned to Chicago. I began my junior year of college, and Saul resumed his routine of writing and teaching. But his finances were permanently altered by the success of *Herzog*. Soon after its publication, I sat silently through a conversation in Yiddish between Saul, my uncle Sam, and my aunt Jane. Fresh from my high school German, I knew that Saul was telling them about the thousands of dollars that were pouring in.

Part of Susan's appeal to Saul was her promise to take care of the practical details he hated. Susan, who did not relish domestic chores, hired a good-hearted woman named Gussie to take care of Daniel and keep house. But her lavish tastes and Saul's newly acquired wealth soon infiltrated their new lifestyle. They bought a co-op apartment facing a lovely park on the shore of Lake Michigan. White plush carpets were installed throughout, and the apartment's eleven rooms were filled with fancy furniture and modern art. The room designated as Saul's study had floor-to-ceiling mirrors on all four walls. Many of his friends thought the mirrors were Susan's idea, symbolizing her desire to bask in Saul's glory and fame, but in fact they were already there when Susan and Saul moved in.

I was raised by a frugal mother and a father who had no steady income until I was eighteen. I never suffered privation, but there was always a lot of anxiety about money along with contempt for the kind of ostentation my uncle Morrie personified. I found the trappings of wealth in their new apartment so repellent that I complained bitterly to Saul. He said that they were of no interest to him, and that wealth did not stop him from writing. "We both know," he ended, "that writing is what I truly care about." As I always had, I accepted what he said about art at face value, but took to visiting Saul in his barren office on the fifth floor of the social sciences building.

When he realized I was staying away from the fancy co-op, he accused me of coming over only when I wanted a check. I told him to mail me the checks, sarcastically adding that when I did come over it was because I wanted to be there! The coercive and divisive influence of money in the Bellow family was never far from my mind, as threats to disinherit had been Abraham's instrument of control. The connection between money and the power of parents over children remained strong in the next generation of Bellows. No doubt my avoidance of that financial trap explained why in later years Saul always spoke glowingly of my financial independence.

By acting like Morrie, the oldest son who forswore his father's promised inheritance, I was trying to sow the seeds of an emotional independence I equated with not taking a cent from either parent. When I graduated from college, I told Saul that the June check was to be the last. Fortunately, I was able to pay for graduate school by combining a scholarship with summer earnings. I did not fully realize until Saul's death that by avoiding the erosive effects of his newfound wealth, I was also trying to maintain a link with the artistic and moral values that prevailed as I grew up.

It did not take long for Saul's marriage with Susan to sour. He was unhappy with her social agenda and the hours she spent playing tennis at the faculty's Quadrangle Club. One of his first complaints was that the tennis was making her "too muscular," but he was more irritated by the lifestyle, which he would take to task in *Humboldt's Gift*. The most serious marital frictions arose when Susan's plans to "civilize" Saul began to include life changes such as leaving Chicago for a more cosmopolitan city like New York or London. Over the years several people told me that she even urged Saul to stop writing, a request that was tantamount to asking my father to stop breathing. By the time I began at the University of Chicago's School of Social Service Administration in the fall of 1966, the atmosphere in their apartment had turned poisonous. A stony silence prevailed at the dinner table. But it was not until the marriage was deteriorating that he started to complain about their opulent surroundings and Susan's spending habits, infuriating me because Saul had defended her when I made exactly those complaints a few years earlier.

As their marriage spiraled downward, Susan urged Saul to see Dr. Heinz Kohut for what turned out to be a brief stint of therapy. Troubled by yet another marital failure, Saul began to weep during the session. My father told me that Dr. Kohut pushed a box of Kleenex forward, commenting that there should be no more of that! After Dr. Rayfield's encouragement of the uninhibited expression of emotions, Saul was dismayed now that he was being urged to control himself. Not surprisingly, he stopped the sessions.

Three-year-old Daniel was very upset by his father's departure, and this was compounded when Susan fired Gussie, who had become a luxury she could no longer afford. Fond of my cute little brother, I continued to visit them. Dan took to expressing his distress by peeing on the white carpets I so hated, and I have to admit that the yellow stains on them greatly pleased me.

Saul came to enjoy affluence in his own way. He hired a tailor named Armando to make his suits, which always featured colorful silk linings. My graduation present from college was one of Armando's suits, although I chose a conservative lining. Some years later, at Adam's wedding, we were joking about the suits and, to prove my point, I went over and exposed the paisley lining of our father's jacket. He also started buying custom shoes from a shop in London that had wooden lasts of my father's feet.

When Saul moved out he was determined that his new apartment be furnished in better taste than the co-op Susan now occupied. He took unusual care in the selection of his furniture, and purchased a fancy Oriental rug and a Mercedes. Susan continued to drive their white Chevy around Hyde Park for years, which Saul attributed to her desire to shame him for withholding money. Bent on making Saul pay for leaving her, Susan used their joint credit cards to force him to pay for whatever she bought, and she proved to be a formidable adversary in court. Charges and countercharges flew back and forth. Several legal cases went on for years, becoming incredibly expensive, and Daniel was eventually dragged into court, much to his detriment. According to Saul, a series of legal teams did not satisfy him. They were no doubt hampered by his custom of expecting quick, positive results. Saul's increasing wealth allowed him to hire wave after wave of lawyers and financial advisers who each in turn were fired, vilified, and then replaced by willing teams who suffered their predetermined fate.

Alone after their separation, Saul rekindled friendships with earthy pals from the old neighborhood whom Susan found objectionable as well as friends around Hyde Park. Dick Stern was a frequent late-afternoon and evening companion who blundered by encouraging Mark Harris to become Saul's biographer. Harris's *Saul Bellow, Drumlin Woodchuck*, published in 1980, is his account of how my father, no doubt flattered and amused, led his hopeful biographer on a merry chase. Obviously Saul wanted no part of the project but was incapable of directly refusing. Instead he emulates his favorite rodent, the woodchuck, who, when it perceives danger, disappears into a burrow that has enough exits to ensure a ready escape. It was an apt description of my father's indirect style of communication; he simply absented himself rather than saying a hurtful no directly to Harris.

In *Drumlin Woodchuck* Harris catalogs the flood of Saul's attractive women companions just after his breakup from Susan. Saul disliked evenings spent alone in Hyde Park and felt a keen desire to reaffirm his sex appeal at fifty-five. Sam Freifeld and Dave Peltz, his old pals from Humboldt Park, introduced him to available women. These casual liaisons occurred when I wasn't around, but once Saul rushed me out of his apartment so he could prepare for "some guests." As I left, I saw Dave walking down the street joking affably with two women in tow. My father would have called them "suicide blondes," as such women, Saul punned, had "dyed by their own hand."

The intellectual companionship afforded by the university also appealed to Saul, notably the crusty Edward Shils. The three of us often walked through a dangerous neighborhood to a dreary Chinese restaurant under the Sixty-third Street El. For reasons that escaped me, both men liked the place, which was staffed by waiters in ill-fitting tuxedos. Edward called the restaurant "the Chinks." When I complained to Saul about what a

sign of prejudice this was, my father, always loyal to the friend
or wife who was currently in favor, defended him. Eventually
Edward and Saul fell out. I do not know the details of their
disagreements, but years later when I was visiting my father in
Boston, Philip Roth called him to ask about his relationship
with Edward. I overheard Saul say that he could not tolerate
Edward's trying to control his thinking. Saul's breaking free of
the powerful intellect of a pure rationalist like Edward appears
to come from a resistance to control that is also apparent in
many of his novels, most notably *Augie March*. But while he
frequently severed ties when he felt too controlled by someone
as forceful as Edward or by wives who made demands he didn't
want to fulfill, he waited to complain until after decadelong
relationships had soured; these complaints were largely for public consumption and to disguise how dependent Saul had felt.
In one such instance that involved Alexandra, his fourth wife,
Saul and Morrie were fighting over the financial proceeds of a
real estate deal in which my father had invested with his older
brother. Alexandra offered to go to Florida to mediate and try
to make peace between the brothers. At the time Saul extolled
her offer as an act of nobility, but after their marriage fell apart
Saul reversed course, complaining bitterly about her greed as
they were negotiating a settlement, completely ignoring his previous praise.

Saul also reconnected to Chicago and a neighborhood structure that he found sustaining. He met my girlfriend, now wife,
while I was in graduate school. After about ten minutes of
conversation, Saul asked if JoAnn had been raised in West Rog-
ers Park, a Chicago neighborhood. Shocked and a little irritated, she asked how he had figured it out. Saul said, "I've made

a study of Chicago accents, neighborhood by neighborhood. I could tell by the way you pronounce certain words."

Along with fortune came fame. Initially refusing to become what he called a "ribbon cutter," someone who presides over public cultural events, Saul gained a reputation for being public-ity shy. But the public eye also appealed. He enjoyed readings, any opportunity to joust with reporters, to respond to critics, and to make known his views on cultural and social issues. Symbolic of his status, Saul had a bit part in Woody Allen's movie *Zelig* where he, the child psychoanalyst Bruno Bettelheim, and Irving Howe, author of *The World of Our Fathers*, were cast as three con-temporary Jewish wise men. Dissatisfied with the script, he re-wrote his dialogue before filming. Saul was also made a Chevalier des Arts et Lettres by the French government. He proudly wore the ribbon for decades until encountering a Frenchman with an identical one in his lapel. When Saul discovered the man's award was for raising prize pigs, his ribbon disappeared.

A long line of admirers now flocked to my father's door. Brent Staples, a young black man from Hyde Park, wanted to meet my father and published a strange account of trying to approach him. Mystified by Staples's quandary, Saul wondered why he didn't simply call and make an appointment with his secretary. But I found Staples's awe an illustration of how Saul's public persona had taken on a mythical quality, drawing people who were interested because he was famous, and feeding his already substantial self-centeredness. And Saul was not blind to the price of fame and how it interfered with the honest give-and-take that characterized his early friendships and rivalries with respected peers like Isaac Rosenfeld, Alfred Kazin, and

dozens of other intellectuals. After the art critic Harold Rosen-
berg died, Saul said he most missed the sound of Harold's voice on
the phone excoriating him with "I can't believe the latest crap
you just wrote."

Humboldt's Gift, published in 1973, even before he won the
Nobel Prize, is my father's literary meditation on the fame that
"good" fortune brings and on the two meanings of "culture"
in American society. Von Humboldt Fleisher, a poet destroyed
by modern life, pickets the opening of a play by his old friend
Charlie Citrine, who has achieved critical and financial success.
Humboldt accuses Citrine of modeling the play's main character after him and exploiting their treasured ideas about
spreading high culture. Citrine's success stands in stark contrast to Humboldt's failure and his later anonymous death. The
danger for the poet in America is voluntary isolation from society, a painful but necessary self-exclusion that can contribute to
the frequent madness of poets, who are too often celebrated, if
at all, after death. The opposite danger is of being smothered by
architects and psychiatrists anxious to rub shoulders with cultural heroes at cocktail parties. Meditating on Humboldt's fate
and upon his own commercial success, Citrine confesses to having been seduced by consorting with the enemy they had both
once despised: the rich, successful Philistines with no real commitment to culture.

Humboldt's Gift mirrors the decline and death of Delmore
Schwartz. Delmore's health had spiraled downward as his sub-
stance abuse grew out of control. He lived with Isaac Rosenfeld's
widow, Vasiliki. Her son George, even as a young adolescent,
understood that Delmore was mad but found his antics amusing. During Delmore's last years, Saul, flush with fame, saw his

decrepit friend on the street in New York and hid, a shameful act to which he confessed in the novel.

The 1972 suicide of Saul's dear friend John Berryman also confirmed his view of the price poets pay. Soon after Berryman's death, we were at a dinner given by the McCloskys in Berkeley. Saul spoke with Ellen Sigelman, a good friend of Berryman's in Minneapolis, about his suicide. My father said he could easily understand why John would not want to stay in this world. What he could not comprehend was how he could turn his back on *King Lear*—that is, on art.

I understood that writing is hard work whether the results are poems or novels. I remember seeing Saul, winter and summer, emerge from his study with his shirt soaked through with sweat. The physical and mental toll that writing took on my father was like the effect of climbing an electric pole, taking hold of the high-tension wires, and letting the current run through him for a long, long time. Saul occasionally quipped, "It was safer to be addicted to sex." He meant that sex was a more favorable vice for a writer than the alcohol that plagued John Berryman, Ralph Ellison, and Delmore Schwartz, and the high price his friends paid for their devotion to writing.

My deep respect for Saul and his writer friends fueled the fierce way I tried to protect his privacy and my acceptance of the line he drew between art and life. As a result, I was predisposed to react negatively to Saul's fame and it got worse when it spilled over onto me. Soon after the publication of *Herzog*, I went over to visit Saul and Susan. As I walked through the lobby of their fancy Chicago apartment building, I nodded a friendly hello to the doorman. When he let me pass without calling upstairs, another tenant asked him who I was. "Oh, that's

Mr. Bellow's son," he told her. She turned to me and said in a snooty tone, "There's no reason to be rude, Mr. Herzog."

I considered Saul and Anita's long-held left-wing political attitudes to be closely intertwined with permissive child rearing, minimal discipline, and encouragement of my independence that characterized our family ethos. Certainly the ethos came from both parents, but Anita remained more militant than Saul. In 1959, at my junior high school graduation, Anita had refused to stand for the national anthem, and Saul chided her for an excessive demonstration of her radicalism. The tenets of our family included a deep appreciation for art and culture, outright contempt for the kind of ostentation Morrie represented, a complete lack of religious observance, sympathy with people who had been disadvantaged or suffered discrimination, support of organized labor in that we did not cross picket lines, respect for people of all races, and a commitment to fairness embodied in the socialist ideal of each according to their needs. Anita expressed that ethos in her work, first in Paris with refugees, then by running a Planned Parenthood clinic, and finally by working for single-payer health plans that she considered socialized medicine.

At ten I knew all about Margaret Sanger and birth control. After my brief foray into capitalism, by sixteen I was committed to world socialism. At seventeen I had decided on a career as a lawyer for the NAACP. I went so far as to find a program that would allow me to finish college and get a law degree in five years. Anita looked at the curriculum and vetoed my plan, insisting I get a general education first. For several years I had envied the intellectual sophistication of my parents and their

University of Chicago–educated friends. By the time I was eighteen, I came to agree with my mother. I set my heart on the university because I wanted more than anything else to be able to think like them and was willing to study hard to ensure I'd be admitted. My career as a socialist ended after I fell asleep during a lecture on Marxist dialectical materialism, and soon thereafter I dropped my interest in the law. But I left Chicago in 1968 committed to the adage of my generation that if you're not part of the solution, you're part of the problem, an adage by which I have lived and in which I continue to find great merit. I never heard a word contrary to the spirit of that adage from my mother or, before 1968, from Saul.

Anita actively encouraged my radicalism, buying me books on Sacco and Vanzetti and the Russian Revolution for birthdays and Hanukkah. My father's friends were former Trotskyites, and he was even afraid of being called to testify before Joseph McCarthy's HUAC, but his politics were not as easy to pin down as they once had been. I take the optimism that pervades his 1948 novel, *The Victim*, to confirm "young Saul's" view that we are all our brothers' keepers.

Within the prevailing family ethos it is easy to understand how the civil rights protests, the Vietnam War, and the turmoil in American society during the mid- and late 1960s came up during my long conversations with Saul in his university office. We supported the civil rights movement but disagreed about the escalating conflict in Vietnam. I felt the United States was involved in an immoral war. Saul made the subtle argument, typical of an immigrant who had been welcomed by this country, that America was a good society that offered its citizens freedom, which made its government worthy of their support. Saul was not perturbed when I joined members of my generation in protest rallies in Chicago and Washington, D.C., or even when I made arguments against participation in the war. But when my refusal to cooperate put my welfare at risk, our arguments got more heated. The force behind our disagreements abated when I got into graduate school to study social work, which extended my draft deferment and temporarily reduced both of our anxiety.

In 1968, as my education neared completion and the war in Vietnam was raging, my options boiled down to two unpleasant prospects: Canada or jail. Saul didn't like the idea of moving to Canada, but he was repelled by the idea of my going to jail, where he feared I would come to harm by violence or as the victim of homosexual rape. As our arguments became more vehement I loudly reminded him that he was once a man whose bookshelf included the works of Gandhi. Often I stormed out of his new apartment in a huff, leaving my father in a rage.

Postadolescent arguments with Saul and Anita were actually a prelude to the candid conversations I began to have with both of them during graduate school, conversations that continued for the rest of their lives. Saul's regular inquiries into my inner life played a pivotal role in my thinking deeply about my feelings and taking my own opinions seriously. What we came to call our "real conversations" gradually shifted away from his recurrent explanations about divorcing my mother to a reciprocal honesty that signaled his recognition of my adult status.

Our talks were certainly not as introspective as my therapy, but they were honest, direct, and psychological in the way Saul used the word: filled with examples of irony, logical contradiction, and runaway vanity as parts of the human comedy, and mortality. They were about what Saul called "the bare facts" and often ended with shared bafflement at human behavior. It was not what Saul said that I treasure. It was what he confessed to not understanding, questions without good enough answers, that made me feel close to him because we were puzzled together.

Our "real conversations" were also a way to resolve conflict, as neither of us could tolerate unresolved ill feelings about each other. Family members were shocked that I'd broach sensitive issues so directly with my father. Forty years of those conversations and my career as a psychotherapist have left me with a deep sense of what is truly important between people: an appreciation for the unvarnished emotional truth, a dislike for mincing words, and a fondness for human folly. The primordial connection between Kenneth Trachtenberg and his uncle Benn Crader in *More Die of Heartbreak* most reminds me of what it felt like to so engage with my father.

The details of any one conversation blend with the others, as they were so regular a feature of our visits. But a snippet about death after my cousin Lynn Bellows, Morrie's daughter, passed away so captures their directness that it remains fixed in my memory. Saul had received a call from his frightened niece as she was being wheeled into surgery. Lynn said, "I love you, Uncle Saul," and, he continued, "I said I loved her, too . . . She must have been afraid of not making it," he then mused. "Absolutely," I responded. "She was staring at her own death right in the face."

My anger at Anita for failing to pay her half of my college expenses had abated, and our arguments stopped. I visited her in South Pasadena, where we also began to have long talks in her beloved garden that are my happiest adult recollections of her.

Over coffee and the soft French cheese that was one of her dietary indulgences, we spoke about my life, her new life in California, our careers as social workers, and the values we shared of seeking the truth, treating people fairly, and social justice.

But I was to make a crucial refinement in our family value of directly facing the truth. With the help of the psychoanalysis I undertook once I moved to San Francisco, I began to hold stating *emotional* truth as a central value, an addition to the family ethos that made both of my parents uncomfortable. Anita avoided her deepest emotions. She was well aware of her reserve and it sorely distressed her. And I was critical of her when she didn't offer the comfort or reassurance I sought. Saul battled harder with all of his confusing emotions. Despite his lifelong inability to manage the effects of tender human feeling, it was at the core of my father's being. Rather than fight my soft side, as my parents did, I eventually came to actively cultivate it in myself, to see its value in my life, and to use it in my work.

Luckily, when my graduate school studies ended and the draft approached, I secured a rare commission in the United States Public Health Service working in a hospital in San Francisco where I felt that I could serve returning casualties from Vietnam in good conscience. Anita said I had fallen into a *schmaltz gribble*, a Yiddish term for a sweet fat spot in life. Saul was relieved that I had avoided jail or Canada and was perfectly happy that I was living in San Francisco until it became clear that I had no intention of returning to Chicago.

The turmoil of the late sixties and its aftereffects on society and in academia caused a gradual though massive personal and political shift in Saul that profoundly and permanently altered our relationship. Within the context of our family ethos I characterized the changes in him as political, though we rarely discussed electoral politics. The shift involved positions he eventually took in the battles over culture—demands for power by groups openly angry about their ongoing disenfranchisement. Its personal side involved Saul's return to his Jewish roots in public and in private, along with a shift in generational attitudes I characterize as a reversal from the position of a rebellious son to those of a patriarchal father. In the dozens of arguments between us, and in long diatribes I endured, most often in private, the personal and the political seemed inseparable in his mind and in mine.

The outlines of reversals to come, of which Saul gave no verbal hint to me, can clearly be seen in *Mr. Sammler's Planet*, his novel about blinding yourself and awakening to the full implications of painful truths. My father shared several forms of blindness with his narrator, Artur Sammler. Like Artur and many Jews, my father kept his eyes closed to the full horror of the Holocaust for two decades. But there were also forms of shared blindness that began well before the Holocaust: the prewar excess of optimism fed by a utopian ideology about the betterment of mankind; the excess vanity of talented young men lauded by their peers and friends; and the disavowal of their Jewish origins as the two ambitious men sought to widen their cultural horizons and gain acceptance.

My father rarely mentioned the Holocaust before the 1967 Arab-Israeli war broke out. But Saul immediately asked Bill Moyers, then publisher of *Newsday*, to secure him press credentials so he could cover the war as a journalist. After I called him

several times and got no answer, I learned that he was in Israel.
When Saul returned, I was angry and complained about his
disappearing without warning and exposing himself to such
danger. His answer was simply "I had to go."

Artur Sammler undertakes an identical journalistic assign-
ment where firsthand exposure to the sights, sounds, and smells
of war's death and decay and to the threat of a second Holocaust
via the destruction of Israel brings home to him, as it did to my
father, the full horror of the Holocaust and of modern life as no
political argument or logical construct could ever do.

The social nightmare to which Mr. Sammler awakens is the
deterioration of New York, which Saul fears is a harbinger of
man's perilous future on earth as humans prepare to set foot on
the moon. Saul's causal explanation for the breakdown in social
order was that the excessive hope and optimism about human
nature he shared with radicals of his generation had grown like
a cancer into the unbridled freedom of the late 1960s.

Anarchy on the street is mirrored by private forms of disorder, the breakdown of authority within the family that needs to
be reasserted. Mr. Sammler takes a dim view of an often dis-
obedient younger generation, favoring only those children who
comply with his wishes. The extensive debt children owe their
parents emerges as Elya Gruner, an overly indulgent father, lies
on his deathbed. Outside his hospital room, Mr. Sammler pres-
sures Elya's daughter to apologize while she still can for the sexual
transgressions that so upset her father. Perhaps more egregious
is the heartless way Mr. Sammler nips his daughter's love in
the bud simply because he thinks the object of her infatuation
will make a poor match, and that she complies with barely a
whimper!

Some people become more politically conservative as they age and often rue their misspent youth. Others, like my mother and her older sisters, do not. But the solution implied in *Mr. Sammler's Planet*, according to the newly minted "old Saul," is a restoration of generational authority. In life, my father's assertion of authority he hadn't previously wielded ushered in friction and acrimony between the two of us that played out for the rest of his life. It was a decade after the publication of *Sammler* before the battle lines were drawn in the culture wars and before "old Saul's" social pessimism took full hold of him. But I rebelled against Saul after his support for the younger generation, whose questioning of established forms of knowledge my father had advocated in life and in his novels, was replaced with demands for respect and compliance with elders who now knew what was best for everyone—elders who had drawn the United States into an immoral war.

I had not met Alexandra Bagdasar Ionescu Tulcea before she married Saul. An established mathematician when they met, Alexandra was born and raised in Romania. Her father, Dumitru Bagdasar, was a neurosurgeon trained in the United States by the famous Harvard neurosurgeon Dr. Harvey Cushing. Her mother, Florica, was a child psychiatrist. Her parents had met in medical school, and both walked the political tightrope between their dedication to patient care and their roles as health ministers in a totalitarian state.

Alexandra was born in 1935, and her father died when she was eleven. After Dumitru's death, Florica, apparently as punishment for accepting help from the Allies during World War II, became politically persona non grata. Life for mother and daughter became precarious. Alexandra then studied mathematics and married a former teacher. In 1957 her husband was offered the rare opportunity to participate in a special research program in the United States. The couple left for Yale University, determined not to return.

By the mid-1970s she was a professor of mathematics at Northwestern and a divorcée. I am not sure whether Alexandra's dissimilarities to Saul's previous wives, including not being Jewish and having a deep commitment to her career, played a role in his decision to marry her. But he must have been unsure about his next step. Before marrying Alexandra, Saul made an impulsive proposal of marriage to Edith Tarcov. Mercifully, she declined.

When I learned about Alexandra's career, one that required hours spent alone, immersed in her own form of abstraction, I hoped that her singular passion for mathematics would be a good fit with my father's life as a writer. After they married, Saul brought Alexandra to California to introduce me to her. I was already married to JoAnn and had a baby daughter, Juliet. Saul was excited by the prospect of a new generation of Bellows and told me that Juliet made him feel part of the continuity of the human race. On subsequent visits, Alexandra and Juliet stole off to a local shopping center for hot chocolate and shopping sprees. Alexandra would hole up in a back room of our house for hours, and when she left the floor would be strewn with sheets of paper covered with abstract mathematical symbols. When I asked if she wanted them, she always said no.

Saul moved to Chicago's North Side, where Alexandra owned an apartment overlooking Lake Michigan. Finding the space too confining, she bought the adjoining apartment, which allowed them both to have studies where they could pursue their intellectual interests without distraction. Alexandra was a very private person. Saul, who prized his privacy while working, missed the companionship he had found in Hyde Park after his writing day was done. Saul joined Alexandra at professional conferences, but conversing with quirky high-level mathematicians was not sufficiently sustaining for him.

Maintaining a geographic distance from Saul was the first in what became a series of insulating layers that afforded me some protection from his demands for attention and control. When rural Vermont became a summer destination for Saul and Alexandra, we trekked there while Juliet was young. On the way to swim in a local pond, our three-year-old little girl joyfully bounded ahead of the grownups. Saul turned to Alexandra and called his granddaughter "a delicious little girl." But sitting around all morning and keeping a lively child quiet while my father wrote and Alexandra did academic work reminded me of my childhood boredom. Eventually I balked at such family vacations and stopped making the effort, placing yet another barrier between us.

Saul put up barriers too, most often with critical judgments that upset me. On occasions when I felt strongly, however, I disagreed and even openly defied his wishes. When I married JoAnn in 1970, I invited all of the doting Goshkins and Saul, but none of the other Bellows—all of whom had ignored me during my childhood—to my small, self-financed wedding. Saul was sore as a boil and complained bitterly at having his family snubbed, being outnumbered by Goshkins, and seeing Anita happily settled in Los Angeles with Basil while he was between marriages.

But Saul always exerted more influence on me than I wished. More often than not, I went along with a man who always argued his viewpoints cogently. But by my late twenties I had tired of judging myself by his standards, although I was never completely free from being hurt by his displeasure, whether it was expressed, implied, or conveyed by others.

Saul had an amazing capacity to make his wishes crystal clear without saying a word. Mysteriously, he was, I believe, able to transform a desire to please others into a capacity to elicit behavior from them that pleased him. (Since I felt that pressure so often, I easily recognized it.) Usually people simply acted as he wished, but frequently they took the extra step of speaking for him without being asked to do so. Surrounded by a cadre of people all too willing to carry what were portrayed as his messages, my father protected himself from delivering bad news, from the danger of being directly refused, or from talking to people with whom he was angry. As a result, there was always a background "buzz" around him.

Unhappy with being on the receiving end of his indirect communication, I stopped his spokespeople in their tracks by insisting that I "accept no substitutes for my father." My brother Adam was too young to take that option. During Saul's long, bitter legal battle with Daniel's mother, Susan, our father did everything he could to avoid speaking with her. When he wanted to talk to Daniel, he would call Adam to deliver the message that his father wanted to speak to him.

But my persistent father would not give up when thwarted. When rational argument and indirect communications failed, Saul destructively took to complaining about people behind their backs. Chronically irritated by my relative independence and their three daughters—were at the same hotel. Alexandra's mother and her aunt were given permission by the Romanian government to attend.

Saul worked on his acceptance speech in the hotel for hours. He took the public forum offered by the award as an opportunity to deliver a message about literature as the gateway to man's beleaguered soul. Quoting Joseph Conrad's preface to *The Nigger of the "Narcissus,"* Saul read that art is an " 'attempt to render the highest justice to the visible universe.' " He continued quoting Conrad, saying that the artist appeals " 'to that part of our being which is a gift and not an acquisition . . . to the latent feeling of fellowship with all creation—and to the subtle but invincible conviction of solidarity . . . which binds together all humanity— the dead to the living and the living to the unborn.' "

Saul contrasted the public attention to the monetary component of the Nobel Prize with the lesser interest expressed in his books as yet another symptom of the elevation of money over culture. Several times he complained about his privacy being invaded, as it was by the traditional St. Lucia ceremony, where a girl with a crown of candles entered their bedroom to serenade Saul and Alexandra. There is a very cute picture of Saul's fellow Nobel laureate, the economist Milton Friedman, in pajamas looking out of his door to find the source of the singing. Later, my father told me the only thing he enjoyed about the week in Stockholm was a quick visit to August Strindberg's study on his way out of town.

Just before we left for the ceremony, I told Saul how proud I was of him. The presentation ceremony, reception, banquet, and ball were elegant. The men were dressed in rented ties and tails, and I joked that I could have passed as a headwaiter at any

from his influence, he complained about me to my l
my wife, and eventually my daughter. JoAnn had al
relationship with Saul after she refused to listen to h
plaints about her husband. But Saul had little use for a d;
in-law who did not side with him. For years, Daniel c
me to our father, though my brother never specified tl
which I was guilty. But I knew what it was: I had grov
ciently far from Saul to have established an independ
The messages my kid brother was to deliver were als
disguised cautions to Dan. He was not to follow in f
that led away from our father.

The apex of the convergence between fame and fort
curred when Saul was awarded the Nobel Prize in 197
sent him a telegram affirming her long-held faith in hi
She added that she knew Lescha, Abraham, and Sonia (
also would have been proud. I went to Stockholm for th
festivities, which turned out to be a grand party. Ou
was assigned a majordomo and a chauffeured limousin
us to a host of receptions and celebrations. Saul and Al
had a suite in the Grand Hotel, and I had a room on th
side of their sitting room. Adam, then about twenty, ar
about twelve, shared a nearby room. Adam and Harrie
serman, my father's literary agent, were chiefly respons
keeping Dan under control, but he still managed to
great deal of food from room service, which infuriate
when the bill arrived.

Morrie was a conspicuous absentee. I can only surm
he could not abide being eclipsed by his kid brother. The
the Bellow party—Jane, Sam, Nina, Lesha, Lesha's hu

fancy restaurant. The recently crowned queen of Sweden, a former German beauty queen, far outshone the king, who for a moment stood alone during the reception. I felt a rough pull, was dragged over to His Highness, and was told to make conversation. Later, Count Something-or-other, the man who had grabbed me, apologized and explained that it was not seemly for the king to have no one with whom to speak. After the ball, Saul, Alexandra, and her mother and aunt were driven back to the hotel. The driver forgot to come back for the rest of us. With Sam's whole family freezing and damp, I approached another limousine driver, who took us to the hotel. My father praised my taking care of them, calling it an act of family feeling, a phrase that he used as a remnant of immigrant life in Lachine.

My brief exposure to the full glare of fame had its pleasures, but I soon became outraged by it. As we entered an event, a reporter shouted a personal question at Saul. Without thinking, I blurted out, "My father's books are in the public domain. He is not." Alexandra, pleased, congratulated me on being "a fighter." At one Stockholm reception, a pleasant man engaged me in what seemed like a friendly chat about families, mostly his. Across the large room a young woman was engaging Adam in a similar conversation. Two days later we found our unguarded comments in the Swedish version of *People* magazine. I was furious, but Saul merely cautioned us to watch what we said. I felt betrayed by the reporter's dishonesty and was determined to keep my relationship with my father strictly private from then on. Adam, also distressed, had a set of T-shirts made up for the whole family that read NOBEL SAVAGES, in part a nod to a literary journal called the *Noble Savage* that Saul had edited more than a decade earlier, but also to the savagery to which we were all exposed.

Saul had expressed concern that winning the Nobel Prize would impair his writing, as he felt the work of previous winners had dropped off significantly after the award. Ted Hoffman sent a letter of congratulation that touched on those fears, expressing a preference for the vitality, freshness, and curiosity of Augie March and Moses Herzog over the darkness of Artur Sammler. Ted told me he thought Saul had been carried away by his own fame. But Ted's letter drips with envy and self-pity couched in faint praise. The letter hurt and angered my father, who ended his long friendship with Ted.

During the twelve-year span that began with the 1964 publication of *Herzog* and ended with the awarding of the Nobel Prize, the idealistic "young Saul" became the pessimistic "old Saul." I cannot fully explain the changes that were brewing in my father. *Mr. Sammler's Planet* hints at how the political tumult of the late sixties affected Saul, and *Humboldt's Gift* addresses the downsides of the fame and fortune that reached a crescendo in Stockholm. From my viewpoint it was during these pivotal years that the optimism and hope I loved and admired in "young Saul" were buried under anger, bitterness, intolerance, and preoccupations with evil and with his death, which lasted for the rest of his life.

More than anything else I attribute the changes to disillusionment and disappointment—disillusionment that the Marxist ideas in which he had placed so much faith had become a rationale for murderous totalitarian dictatorships, and disappointment in the failure of art to transform the world into a less materialistic place, a place where the human solidarity of which

Conrad writes about might have nourished a second Renaissance.

But by then, nearing forty, I had to find a way to live with the "old Saul" who emerged in the late 1970s, a man who had lost his faith in the ability of collective action to better mankind and had adopted his father's stance of paternal authority I found excessive. What I have come to see as a thirty-year cold war between my father and me was a struggle between two men with antithetical attitudes toward both social change and generational compliance who were also two men who loved one another and sought to keep their relationship alive.

"OLD SAUL":
THE LITERARY PATRIARCH

Chapter Eight

A FAILURE AT SPIRITUALITY:
1977–86

A FTER THE FESTIVITIES in Stockholm, Saul was particularly fatigued in spirit when he returned to Chicago. Even the spiritual ideas of Rudolf Steiner, the Austrian philosopher Saul had studied for a number of years, who held complex notions about the possibility of an expanded consciousness that continued after physical death, were proving insufficient to ward off his deepening pessimism.

Steiner claimed to be a clairvoyant and had developed a theory of an evolving consciousness that included individual and collective memories as well as past, present, and, most crucial to Saul, future lives. The possibility of *spiritual* self-improvement offered Saul a way to try to cleanse his soul, an antidote to the contamination wrought by fame and fortune. My father found little solace in organized religion, but he had a lifelong preoccupation with death. Steiner claimed that anyone who takes the time and effort to develop their faculties can gain such expanded capacities. In private, Saul put Steiner's meditative techniques into regular practice for years. Steiner's books were all over his apartment, left open and upside down, as if he had just paused after reading a passage.

At Saul's recommendation I read a few of Steiner's complex books and it became clear to me that the idea of the human soul returning, over and over, in a more refined state of enlightenment held a great appeal to a man left bereft and lonely after the loss of family and friends. As his interest in Steiner deepened, the phrase *inner life* came to be replaced by the human soul in our conversations, and he infused the term with a spiritual component that convinced me he had come to believe in the soul's immortality. This made me uneasy; I was more comfortable with the idea of a self without transcendental aspects. However, unlike our other disagreements where my father tried to prevail, he was perfectly tolerant of my resistance. I always suspected that Saul's uncharacteristic lack of argumentative ardor reflected his lingering doubts about spirituality.

Saul could not have chosen a greater challenge to his logical abilities than to convince himself of Steiner's ideas about a spiritual life after physical death. The doubts Saul and I shared about what could be explained, including the limits we found in logic, cemented our relationship. I found that view confirmed in several revealing conversations soon after my fortieth birthday. I expressed a brief interest in philosophy and asked Saul to recommend some readings to me, which pleased him. I became puzzled by what seemed to me Hegel's logical contradiction about Napoleon and the end of history, and asked Saul to explain it. He replied, "These guys [philosophers] just think themselves into corners they can't get out of."

I found our shared skepticism about how great thinkers are removed from life's everyday problems most clearly exemplified near the end of *The Adventures of Augie March*. On a sea voyage Augie meets Bateshaw, a philosophical shipmate preoccupied with abstract theories about improving the human condition. After a shipwreck, they are almost drowned until they come upon a lifeboat. Augie helps his companion into the vessel. But as soon as Bateshaw is no longer in danger, he gets so lost in his own thoughts about how to save the world that he fails to help Augie aboard. Implicitly my father is asking how much faith the world can place in any set of ideas when the "great thinkers" are so engaged in finding ways to save mankind that they cannot be bothered to rescue a drowning man.

Several of Saul's friends had strong personal reactions to this passage that illustrate the difficulties in equating literary characters with specific people. More than a few came to believe or were told by "knowledgeable" third parties that they were the model for Bateshaw and expressed irritation to me at being characterized as super-rationalists with their heads in the clouds—or worse. Saul knew many such thinkers, and it was certainly not beyond him to insert a detail so personal as to make it crystal clear to one reader that he had him in mind.

But as tempting as it may be to equate characters with people, only my mother, who found a detail in *Seize the Day* that convinced her that Saul had put it there out of spite, has ever claimed to have found him- or herself directly identified. Though I find eerily familiar descriptions of people, places, and life events, I cannot assuredly form direct equations with real people, with the notable exceptions of my father's narrators. Though their eyes and in their voices I see a lifelong series of emotional snapshots that reveal my father's point of view, his frame of mind, and, most revealing, a novelistic soul-searching rarely present even in our real conversations.

———

By the mid-1970s Saul had renewed his friendship with Hyman Slate, who lived near Saul and Alexandra on Chicago's North Side. On Sunday afternoons they would get together over a pot of tea and talk about all sorts of worldly matters. But the question of immortality soon came to dominate, and they formed a two-man study group dedicated to reading and discussing theories about death and the afterlife.

A few years later Hyman was diagnosed with an aggressive cancer that would quickly claim his life. By then Saul had divorced Alexandra, had married once again, and was living in Boston. My father and I called Hyman to say goodbye. Saul ended the conversation by telling his old friend how much he admired the bravery Hyman showed in the face of death. Some months earlier, I had visited Hyman in Chicago and had found his health already precarious. He expressed a fond desire to reread Isaac Rosenfeld and Saul's Yiddish translation of T. S. Eliot's poem "The Love Song of J. Alfred Prufrock," which had circulated among Saul and Isaac's friends in Hyde Park, including the sociologist Daniel Bell. Moved by Hyman's request, I took it upon myself to secure a copy for him. Daniel Bell's daughter Jordy, an undergraduate classmate at the University of Chicago, told me her father had transcribed the poem from memory, and I quickly forwarded a copy to Evelyn Slate, Hyman's wife, who read it to him on his deathbed. Evelyn told me how much he appreciated hearing her read the poem, and I passed their gratitude on to Saul.

In his 1976 Nobel lecture, Saul had expressed an optimistic view about the universal capacity of art to bind humanity. But just a year later, a dark pessimism that must have been fermenting in him since the late sixties emerged full-blown. In 1977 Saul was invited by the National Endowment for the Humanities to give the Jefferson Lectures, an honor for scholarly contributions. He delivered two stern lectures about the uneasy balance between the fragility of art and the fate of the artist in a materialist American culture that took little notice of either. As the second lecture ended he expressed deep concern about the deterioration of the social and political structures that had nurtured him as a young man and that extended to the fragile state of the entire human endeavor.

In *Mr. Sammler's Planet*, a dark book by any measure, Saul worried that the future of civilized society was at risk. A decade after the defiance of civil authority at the 1968 Democratic Convention, on university campuses, and on the streets, Saul worried that these upheavals might well unravel the traditional bonds that hold society together. Angry objections to inequalities expressed by my generation, by women, and by blacks now in political power posed a threat to the twenty-five hundred years of Western culture Saul had studied and to which he had devoted his life.

In the late 1970s and '80s, Saul began to criticize the growing tide of political correctness in society and began to take conservative positions on matters of race and gender. Saul's refusal to consider the merits of disenfranchised groups seemed a reversal that was out of character, and I was upset to hear views from an increasingly embittered father that diverged from our family ethos of fairness, respect, and concern.

His anger interfered with the subtlety of "young Saul's" arguments, which were replaced by the same kind of dogmatic stridency he had once found objectionable. However, as unfair as I found his arguments to be, I need to make a crucial distinction between the organized groups whose demands for the redistribution of power he resisted and individual blacks and women whom he respected and liked, intellectuals like Ralph Ellison during the 1950s and later Stanley Crouch, a black music critic.

But what stands out are several conversations, initiated by my father during the mid-'60s, about the concerns Saul felt for the dangers faced by Gussie, Saul and Susan's maid, a woman he genuinely liked and whose courage he respected, and her daughters. Gussie was raising two teenage girls who lived in a housing project a short bus ride from Saul's apartment. Her responsibilities entailed serving dinner and cleaning up, and Gussie did not get home until 8:00 P.M. Saul worried that her daughters were exposed to a violence-ridden environment for many hours without Gussie to protect them and that they'd be caught up in a whirlpool that would destroy the girls.

I could never resolve my dislike of the contrast between that personal respect and concern and his cold rejection of demands by populations too long silent of whom I became an unapologetic supporter. Our arguments may well have brought out the worst in my father. Arguing with him only increased his ferocity and prolonged what amounted to tirades. However, even when I refrained from objecting in the hopes of ending painful-to-endure diatribes sooner rather than later, I was appalled at what he said. At times I felt some resistance was necessary: partly to remind him of how he had changed and partly because I was appalled to hear such bile flowing out of the father I loved.

After having lauded the successes of the civil rights movement in the South, Saul took an increasingly negative view of the militancy among blacks in Chicago. Hyde Park was a black ghetto long before his return to the University of Chicago in 1961. Never a safe neighborhood, it was now a place where students were immediately cautioned about where it was safe to walk. An undergraduate was murdered near the campus in 1968, my last year in school. Everyone was frightened and Saul became increasingly cautious and troubled by the urban decay that was destroying the Chicago he fondly remembered.

In the late 1970s Saul tried to escape Hyde Park by moving into Alexandra's apartment on the northern tip of Chicago, but that did not remove him from a city tensely divided along racial lines. By then the once all-white North Side had changed to a veneer of luxury lakefront buildings that was only two blocks deep. My aging father had me walk with him to the local supermarket because he wanted to show me he had to walk through an all-black neighborhood that frightened him in order to buy a bag of groceries.

When black elected officials expressed elation about wielding political power, Saul was furious. And when some of them made anti-Semitic statements, including an accusation that Jewish doctors were spreading AIDS in the African American community, he was outraged. He counterattacked in public, blaming black politicians and journalists for not contradicting these statements. He found an ally and later a friend in the second Mayor Daley, who, citing his status as a lawyer, demanded proof for such inflammatory accusations from the black leaders. Saul thought Daley heroic for taking that stand.

"Old Saul's" reversal of his sociocultural views mirrored changes on a personal and generational level that I found equally if not more objectionable. The once rebellious and irreligious son now found favor in the wisdom of the older generation and in the Jewish roots from which he had distanced himself during my formative years.

I believe my father's anger over black anti-Semitism had become intertwined with generational issues, now also reversed. Given the contribution of Jews to the civil rights movement, the demands of newly enfranchised blacks smacked to him of the ingratitude of spoiled children, now grown, toward the parents who made earlier sacrifices for them. Saul had adopted attitudes much like his father's toward ungrateful children and made snide comments, usually wrapped in humor, about their lack of appreciation for the long-suffering parents who always paid when the bill came due. Even though I paid for my children's orthodontia, Saul could not resist a recurrent though clever bon mot that revealed a deep-seated resentment about generational ingratitude, that went, "The good thing about children having straight teeth is that they leave a clean mark when they bite the hand that feeds them."

An angry Saul ruffled feathers when he served on the board of the MacArthur Foundation. Dissatisfied with the intellectual quality of the work by women and black applicants, he fought against their grants. And Saul offended everyone when he publicly asked, "Who was the Tolstoy of the Zulus?" In a feeble defense, he cited his years as an anthropology student and claimed to be drawing a distinction between literate and preliterate societies. His explanation satisfied no one.

In most respects generations of Bellow men had not viewed women as anything approaching equals. Morrie's daughter Lynn thought herself intellectually inferior to the Bellow men, and Sam's daughter Lesha complained about how poorly the family treated women. When Lesha and her husband, also named

Saul, depressed, in 1952.

Greg as a latchkey kid.

The Bellow family, 1955. Seated: Abraham and Fanny Bellow. Standing left to right: Shael Bellows, Lesha Bellows, Lynn Bellows, Marge Bellows, Morrie Bellows, Jane Kauffman, Samuel Bellows, Nina Bellows, and Joel Bellows.

Bard College Literature Division, 1953. Standing from left: Keith Botsford, Saul Bellow, Irma Brandies, Anthony Hecht, and William Frauenfelder. Seated: Jack Ludwig (center), William Humphrey, Warren Carrier, and Andrus Wanning. (Courtesy of the Bard College Archives and Special Collection)

Alexandra "Sasha" Tschacbasov.
(Courtesy of the late Sasha Bellow)

Greg and Ted Hoffman in Tivoli.

Beebee Freedman Schenk de Regniers.

Susan Glassman.
(Courtesy of Daniel Bellow)

Saul in Aspen.

Saul and Dan.

Alexandra Bagdasar Ionescu Tulcea.
(Courtesy of Alexandra Bellow)

Saul in Stockholm. (AP Images)

The Bellow boys in Stockholm. (Charles Osgood, *Chicago Tribune*)

Edith Tarcov.

Lesha and Sam Greengus. (Courtesy of Lesha Greengus)

Saul at Adam's wedding.

Saul and Janis Freedman Bellow. (Courtesy of Daniel Bellow)

Anita holding court in Pasadena.

Saul in Vermont.

Sam, wanted to send their three bright daughters to the best colleges, her father said it was a waste of good money. While Saul treated Anita very much as an equal in their early years, her independence became a sore point as their marriage soured. And Saul hated Anita's friend Maja because she advocated that women should be as free to sleep around as men.

To say that Saul did not respect individual women disregards the love he felt for many and the trust he placed in several. Harriet Wasserman was his longtime literary agent, and my cousin Lesha was a trusted adviser in his financial dealings for decades. Lesha and Alexandra thought Saul's attitudes toward women got worse when he and Allan Bloom became friends. But Allan, like Isaac Rosenfeld decades earlier, articulated a rationale for self-serving attitudes about gender that justified and even glorified men taking advantage of feminine self-sacrifice that, to me, shows how Saul's social positions bled into personal attitudes to which Saul had long subscribed.

Once again, there were differences between the trust Saul placed in individuals and his enmity for groups and disagreeable beliefs. Saul had little sympathy with feminist ideas, the increasing presence of women in academia, or prominent women writers. When my stepbrother's partner of twenty years, Mary Ryan, was awarded a Bancroft Prize in American History, I mentioned it and Saul commented that she was, no doubt, the most qualified woman, implying that she was given preference because of her gender.

Candace Falk, a former student of Saul's and former director of the collection of the anarchist Emma Goldman's papers, told me a story that perfectly captures Saul's views on militant blacks and women as well as his love for a bon mot. As a graduate student, Candace took Saul's seminar on James Joyce. During that quarter, a student strike was declared in protest over the bombing of Cambodia and the imprisonment of the Black Panther Bobby Seale. Candace approached Saul very politely and requested that he cancel his seminar as a political statement. Later, when she stood before the class and urged them to leave with her and join the strike, Saul shot back, "I'll be damned if I support anything that has to do with Bobby Seale," and added, "The only thing you women's liberationists will have to show for your movement in ten years will be sagging breasts!" Candace left the class insulted and crestfallen.

Saul's objection to blacks and women who were agitating for a voice and a place at the table seemed to me an obvious parallel with the attitudes held within WASP-dominated departments of English about Jews in the 1940s. That he was capable of ignoring this parallel shows how angry Saul was and how the strife over power in academia had so gotten under his skin. By 1982, when he wrote *The Dean's December*, his scorn had come to include the social and racial anarchy he thought had by then thoroughly infected society, and how political correctness had infected the universities.

I found Saul's switch from the position of a rebellious son to that of a patriarchal father the most painful because it entailed a reversal of his attitudes toward authority and an accompanying pressure to conform that was to become a sore point for decades. Long gone was Saul's tolerance of my adolescent backtalk, and an eight-year-old Adam was told "Honor thy father" after trying to speak up for himself. When my daughter Juliet attended college and graduate school on the East Coast in the 1990s, she visited her grandfather. Juliet was eager to engage

Saul in intellectual discussions, but he irritated her by repeat-edly sidestepping her overtures to talk about art and culture and, instead, urged her to marry and start a family before she turned thirty.

Saul's opposition to the younger generation's social anarchy and lack of respect were hardened during a 1968 lecture he gave at San Francisco State, a campus ripped asunder during that tumultuous year. The event made its way, practically word for word, into *Mr. Sammler's Planet*. After the lecture, a member of the audience shouted my father down, characterizing him as old, irrelevant, and impotent. I do not know which was worse for Saul: the attack on his virility, the discounting of his politi-cal relevance, or the fact that no one from the faculty came to his defense. Saul was deeply offended, and the sting stayed with him for years, crystallizing what was already a growing nega-tive feeling about the thoughtless radical left and liberal aca-demics who tolerated such insolence.

A friend who witnessed the scene told me that Saul seemed unable to parry the kind of attack that other academics had to learn to expect and to weather, letting the criticisms get under his skin, responding with anger, and counterattacking. Instead of the positive advocacy for the traditions of Western culture that was sorely needed, Saul's blind anger led him to articulate sociopolitical positions so repellent that even I lost sight of our basic agreement about the value of what dead white men had to say about political life and human experience.

In 1987 Allan Bloom published *The Closing of the American Mind*, in which he argued that overly liberal attitudes had actu-ally closed the American mind in the name of openness. After a careful reading, I found the book so closely paralleled views I

was hearing from my father that I considered it a joint intellectual venture by two friends who had grown ideologically close.
Bloom put forth views that appealed to social, cultural, and political conservatives in the Reagan White House, and Saul did
not protest being included among thinkers with whom he often
agreed. When Saul and I discussed the book I expressed distress
that it was filled with "aristocratic notions." I took his silence
about my characterization as tacit agreement and as a measure
of the extent to which my father's mind had closed to anything
but "superior" forms of culture, an attitude that bordered on
the elitism I found in Allan's book that was the exact opposite
of my understanding of "young Saul's" views. Bloom went after
his enemies in public much as Saul had to me in private, with
venom, ridicule, and contempt designed to obliterate opposing
views rather than to consider any potential worth in them or
offering a contrasting position.

When "young Saul" became "old Saul," my father changed
from a young man full of questions to an old man full of answers. Virtually gone was Saul's early optimism about making
the world a better place. Worse, from my point of view, was the
loss of his puzzlement about human nature, which I shared and
treasured. "Old Saul" now took everything, including himself,
so seriously that he lost the ability to laugh at himself or at the
comic side of life's contradictions. In earlier years, his pointed
questioning of abstract solutions that offered little help to suffering human beings had seemed to me a form of leveling that
brought great thinkers down to earth. My father was now sid-
ing with the thinkers he had once challenged, promulgating a
set of answers and solutions to problems, both social and personal, that I found distinctly patriarchal, authoritarian, and hi-

erarchical. My gut impressions of Saul's reversals—that what he was backing away from was the basic fairness of the family ethos with which I had been raised—never wavered. I was and remain saddened by the toll Saul's disillusionment and pessimism took on him and on us.

In midwinter 1978, Saul and Alexandra hurriedly flew to Bucharest to help her gravely ill mother. Her parents had many former colleagues in the medical community, and Alexandra tried to pull strings in order to secure the help of the doctors her father had trained. The Romanian authorities were bent on making Florica and her daughter, who had escaped to the West, suffer. The government officials adhered to harsh bureaucratic regulations, refusing to call in specialists and limiting family visits. Alexandra's mother died a few days after their arrival. Family and friends helped as much as they could, but it was a bitter experience. When they returned to Chicago, Alexandra fell into a state of nervous exhaustion, and it took months for her to recover fully.

The Dean's December is set in Bucharest, where Dean Albert Corde and his wife, Minna, go to help her dying mother. In the novel my father contrasts the brutality of the Romanian regime that makes it impossible for a woman to die with her family nearby against an equally ghastly series of events in Chicago, where political and social anarchy have eroded the social fabric. Contrasting what Saul called the hard nihilism of the Eastern Bloc and the soft nihilism of the West, he found little fundamental difference in the pervasive evil within human nature under a totalitarian government and in a political system where freedom had run amok.

Despite being in poor health, Basil, Anita's husband, had ambitious retirement plans that included a desire to live at the beach and to travel. Anita was happy to stay in the home they had shared. Work, pottery, her garden, and walks with Basil along the beach they so loved were sufficient for her. Their differences became so pronounced that Basil rented an apartment near the Pacific Ocean, though he stopped by their home after his classes almost every day. At first Anita was upset, but she soon accommodated herself to living alone and to visiting us without her peripatetic husband.

Basil moved back into their home about a year later, but by then his energy and health had waned. In late 1984, he died of a massive stroke in mercifully brief seconds. When I told Saul about Basil's death, he asked whether he should call Anita to offer his condolences. Unsure how she would react, my father feared stirring up Anita's unrequited love for him. Unwilling to push my father to do something he really did not want to do, I left it up to him. He never called, though he should have.

Soon after Basil's death, Anita and I sorted out her finances. She said that for the first time in her life she felt rich and asked me what she should do with the money. Referring to her fantasy about Saul's fame and fortune after their divorce, I joked that she should buy herself a gold Cadillac and drive past Saul's house. That was our final good laugh together.

A few years earlier, Anita had suffered a "silent" heart attack. Though she was not hospitalized, her heart had sustained damage. Basil had to force the usually stoic Anita to tell me about the attack. Within weeks of Basil's death, my mother began an accelerating downward spiral of cardiac illness that soon took her life. A lifelong smoker whose heart was much weaker than

I realized, she could not be stabilized with medications, and surgery was impossible.

On her last day in the ICU, several of her closest friends and I took turns keeping her company. None of us could bear watching her die. There were tubes everywhere, including one that prevented her from speaking. From somewhere deep within me, the right words came. I thanked her for her years of devotion and expressed regret that we seldom spoke aloud about loving one another. I said I knew she loved me, and she nodded her head in vigorous affirmation. Rick and Jeanne Busacca, Basil's children, each said a private goodbye to their stepmother of twenty-five years. After a brief flicker of green light on the monitors, Anita died. I sat alone with her before turning her body over to the hospital staff.

The next day Saul called. My father was at his absolute best as I sobbed into the phone. Saul's tenderness was palpable as he said, "Come to Chicago. Your loving father will be waiting." By then many barriers existed between us, but seeing me suffer always cut through to our fundamental emotional connection. After the loss of my mother, I could better understand Saul's sensitivity to suffering and why death remained a constant thought. When Anita's estate was settled, I tearfully told Saul I missed her so much that I'd gladly forgo every cent for just five minutes with her. "I know," he said.

Three months after Anita's death, Juliet and I went to Chicago to visit Alexandra and Saul. He asked for the details of Anita's final illness, and commented that she had gotten "a quick ticket," meaning that she did not linger or suffer. A few days before we arrived, my uncle Morrie had passed away, and my uncle Sam was on his deathbed in Chicago. The month before,

Saul had visited a terminally ill Morrie at his home in Georgia and offered to return on a moment's notice. But Morrie was hours from death when his second wife, Joyce, called. Saul and his niece Lesha hurried to Georgia. When they arrived, Joyce said, "He's in there," indicating the next room, and both Saul and Lesha were shocked when they found only a jar of ashes. Saul had just returned from Georgia when we arrived, and as my shaken father sat next to Juliet, then about eleven, and stroked her hair, I watched as his granddaughter's touch sustained him.

Sam's prostate cancer had metastasized. He was at home but had stopped eating in order to speed death along. Nina was beside herself. Sam relented and asked for veal Marengo, one of his favorites. Nina insisted that no one tell him that Morrie had died, but Sam, no fool, had gotten the picture when his brother Saul and his daughter Lesha hurried out of town without explanation and when nobody gave him a straight answer when he asked after his older brother's health. Sam died a few weeks later. He was buried in Israel, where he and Nina had lived for part of each year. With Anita, Morrie, and Sam dead, Saul and I were down in the dumps, but, he added, "at least we're down there together!"

The three deaths were the beginning of the end for Saul and Alexandra. After the trip to Romania, her energy had returned, and it appeared to me that they spent a number of happy years together. I particularly remember how much he and I enjoyed explaining American idioms to her. They took a vacation in Spain and returned with elegant capes they wore to a family dinner at their favorite Italian restaurant, where as favored fans of the Chicago Light Opera, Saul and Alexandra often joined the singers and their colorful director for postperformance meals that ran late into the night. During an academic semester they spent in Israel, Alexandra taught and Saul studied the Middle East in preparation for writing *To Jerusalem and Back.*

But the appearance of contentment papered over growing marital frictions. After summering in Vermont for years, they decided to build a vacation home. It quickly became a sore point when Alexandra did not take sufficient interest in the myriad construction decisions, placing those burdens on Saul. Lesha, who vacationed nearby, saw their marriage deteriorate into the same cold war of interminable silences that I had witnessed between Saul and Susan twenty years earlier. During their last few years together, Saul told me that Alexandra's devotion to her career wore on him, but, as he did not want to go through another divorce, he claimed to be reconciled to living in a marriage that lacked warmth.

I do not know when Allan Bloom began meddling directly in Saul and Alexandra's marriage, but he and my father loudly espoused views about gender roles so slanted toward men that they irritated the women who heard them. Alexandra was a professor of mathematics, a field dominated by men, and she was duly proud of her accomplishments. She found Bloom arrogant and came to resent his persistent claims on her husband's favor. She was furious when Allan barged into their bedroom once when she had not finished dressing. Worse, both men trivialized her complaints and Allan made it worse by chalking up her anger to her "conventional attitudes."

The fundamental incompatibilities between Saul and Alexandra are reflected in a scene from *The Dean's December.* In the first private moment between husband and wife after the funeral of Minna's mother, they take a walk in the bitter cold. Though Minna has rejected Corde's physical comfort, she seeks his help in understanding the flood of confusing emotions brought on by her bereavement. Corde knows it is impossible, but he tries to translate a lifetime of his attempts to understand the human condition into the scientific forms of thought Minna uses to understand the physical world. All too soon, his explanation begins to sound like a lecture. Minna, infuriated for a moment, soon comes to see that she has asked the impossible.

Both knew the marriage was all but over, but Alexandra took the final steps to end it that, as usual, my father could not initiate. After they separated, Saul visited me in California. Characteristically, he showed his disappointment by finding an explanation embedded in the material concerns of a defective society. Obviously infuriated by being forced to spend his time on the practical details involved in building a house that Alexandra refused to deal with, after being forced to choose from a catalog filled with bathroom fixtures, Saul railed about American materialism for upwards of fifteen minutes before saying, "Enough of that," and changing the subject.

More fundamentally I understood that the end of their marriage was linked to the three recent deaths that had brought Saul's demise clearly into focus. He had convinced himself that Alexandra lacked the emotional strength to see him through his final passage. I had witnessed a scene in Vermont when she came upon a long-lost letter from her father and was inconsolable. Between that reaction and her collapse after her mother's death, Saul made clear to me his view that she could not contend with his old age and physical deterioration.

Based on my memory of that incident in Vermont, I accepted Saul's rationale and, out of what I considered loyalty to him, kept my distance from Alexandra for a number of years. As it turned out, Alexandra married a mathematician of note, Alberto Calderón, who died before Saul. Contrary to Saul's expectations, she faced Alberto's death with fortitude and rebounded into an active retirement. She and I have long since mended fences.

On that same visit Saul told me he had an open invitation from Stanford's Center for Advanced Study in the Behavioral Sciences to come for a semester and write. The center was right down the road from us, and I encouraged him to accept. I thought a break from Chicago might do him good, and I hoped that more time near my family would generate a better relationship between my father and my children.

Saul's usual routine as he was about to leave was to sing a rendition of Groucho Marx's song "Hello, I Must Be Going" to lighten the moment. But this time he left for Chicago with a parting shot about being where people cared about him. A comment that implied that my family and I were not sufficiently demonstrative to suit Saul, coupled with the absence of the philandering that had followed the end of his first three marriages, were hints that he already had a romantic agenda in place.

Saul's dissatisfaction with the answers offered by spirituality had been growing long before he won the Nobel Prize. In *Humboldt's Gift*, a novel permeated by death consciousness, Saul considers Rudolf Steiner and spirituality in the most depth. His narrator, Charlie Citrine, does regular meditative exercises to clear his mind. But, like my father's, Charlie's mind is too clouded with the material world and a need for human contact to prepare his soul to move on. Knowing that he has failed to right himself, Saul's narrator expresses what I consider my father's implicit acceptance of responsibility for his own spiritual failure. Charlie is nearly resigned to living with his all-too-human shortcomings when the memory of Von Humboldt Fleisher reminds him of the transcendent value of art, which is Humboldt's true gift. In a gift from the great beyond that lightens the sting of physical death, Charlie's deceased friend offers him the hope of another chance to do things right next time around in an existence to come that is free of material distractions and the pain of loss.

As much as my father wished to become more spiritual, Saul knew he could never allow himself to follow Steiner's first instruction to all seekers of spiritual truth: to abandon one's critical faculties and take a leap of faith. Saul's mental and verbal agility allowed him to suppress parts of himself for a time, but his lifelong embrace of reason combined with the undeniable reality of physical death ate away like an acid at his desire to believe in any form of immortality. In the end, Saul found the hope offered by Steiner insufficient to get him through the end of a fourth marriage and his grief over three family deaths in the span of six months.

Saul was equally disappointed in his connections with the living after his fourth marriage failed. The unsuccessful conversation between Corde and Minna in *The Dean's December* shows how well Saul recognized the unbridgeable gap between man and wife but it also highlights a crucial distinction between my father's magnificent descriptive capacities and the inability to explain what cannot be fully understood: the unbridgeable gaps between human beings. Saul's observational capacities and his descriptive abilities have been universally praised. My cousin Lynn remarked on how her uncle Saul captured the experience of walking up the steps to Abraham and Fanny's house, steps she had often trod. In another instance, analogizing Jack Ludwig's body movements to rowing a Venetian gondola is a descriptive triumph, but any description of Jack, no matter how accurate or complete, does not explain how he was able to cast a Svengali-like spell over Sasha and Saul, why Sasha betrayed Saul, or why Saul so trusted his deceitful friend.

Perhaps an explanation for Saul's failed marriages lies in the excessively romanticized notions of love—the same notions Saul chronically complained about in Beebee—held by a man who thought he acted for rational reasons. But it was Saul who was not sufficiently in touch with reality when in love. And when his second and third marriages ended in misery, it was he who claimed "temporary insanity" to Mitzi McClosky, explaining that his courtships of Sasha and Susan occurred when he was finishing a novel and was "half insane." But his first marriage to Anita, which freed him from Abraham's control, and his fourth to Alexandra, a marriage more consciously chosen, ended only slightly less bitterly.

While romanticized expectations may or may not have clouded his judgment, after a fourth marital failure, my father appeared to have nearly given up on finding love. In *More Die of Heartbreak*, published in 1987, the novel's main character, Benn Crader, accepts a life of icy solitude and goes off to the arctic to study a form of lichen that enters a state of dormancy so deep that it appears to be dead. But my father, despite his disappointment, did not give up on love *or* on seeking a path to immortality. He found a new metaphor for the soul's rebirth in the apparent death of lichen that spring back to life when conditions of sufficient physical warmth permit, and he discovered a new source of the human warmth he found so necessary in the selfless love of Janis Freedman.

Chapter Nine

BURYING "YOUNG SAUL" ALIVE:
1987–93

JANIS DOWNPLAYED THE years before she arrived at the
University of Chicago and Saul entered her life. My brother
Adam briefly took graduate classes with her at Chicago. They
became friends, and he reported that Janis was so in awe of her
mentors that she took down every word, including Allan Bloom's
jokes.

Janis was raised in Toronto and has a brother and a sister who
is an astronomer. I have exchanged only a few words with Janis's parents. Her father was a psychoanalyst and an admirer of
Saul's. According to Adam, he urged Janis to pursue a Ph.D. at
the university's Committee on Social Thought, where my father
and Allan Bloom were professors. After some years her studies
hit a snag and she took a position as Saul's secretary; her loyalty
and selflessness were just the traits my father valued.

As their romance developed in private, I heard little about
Janis until a 1986 family wedding, when Saul told me he wanted
to marry a woman forty years his junior. He talked freely about
the sacrifices a young woman makes when she marries a man
over seventy. After the decline and death of his brothers, Saul
was acutely aware that he could soon become a physical burden

to her and that he was depriving Janis of a long marriage and children. Saul also repeated doubts expressed by Lesha and others who explicitly discouraged him from fathering another child. I did not express an opinion about the merits of the marriage, but added my doubts about having a child. Saul readily agreed.

Our one-sided talk ended with him concluding that Janis was a grown woman who understood what she was doing. But he had already made up his mind. Talking over his doubts with me was only an exercise to reduce his guilt over what he knew to be a selfish act. As the marriage became a real possibility, people close to Janis tried to talk her out of this May–December arrangement, but she was unmoved.

I never heard another word from my father about her sacrifice. But *More Die of Heartbreak* is about love and was written as Saul's marriage to Alexandra was ending and his romance with Janis was blooming. The novel's main characters, Benn Crader and his nephew Kenneth Trachtenberg, are mystified by women. Benn, after turning himself inside out for yet another romance, gives up on them. But Kenneth, after pursuing an ex-wife who does not love him, becomes romantically involved with a former student, Dita, who has decided that they are suited for each other and takes the romantic initiative. Dissatisfied with her physical appearance, Dita undergoes painful cosmetic surgery, a procedure during which facial skin is sanded off. As Ken nurses Dita back to health, he finds her sympathetic and straightforward in her desire for him. What I find most personally revealing is that Ken finds, in Dita, the essential ingredients Saul found missing in his previous wives—uncritical acceptance and warmth.

I believe Janis's support was more palatable to Saul than the

forms offered by my mother, Sasha, Susan, and Alexandra. All four previous wives were self-assured women who never appeared daunted by being married to him, who expected a measure of respect for their views and credit for the work involved in keeping a household afloat. The imbalances of age and life experience between Saul and Janis were obvious enough, but he highlighted them by making demands that underscored her compliance; she did every little chore he asked of her. To top it off, Saul adopted "baby" as a term of endearment that, given the disparities, I found disconcerting.

At Saul's request, Lesha arranged a small wedding in Cincinnati attended by Janis's family. Soon thereafter they visited California, where she met me, my family, and Saul's old friends Herb and Mitzi McClosky. Perhaps feeling she needed to justify herself, Janis made her case to Mitzi for marrying a man so many years older, saying that she'd rather be married to Saul for five years than to somebody else for fifty. Janis planned to com plete her stalled dissertation about women in the Roman' literary tradition, such as Madame Bovary and Anna Kareni' who make personal sacrifices for an ideal form of great love no longer exists in our modern world. According to Saul set herself a quota of two pages a day and quickly finish dissertation. He got all dressed up in his full academic g thoroughly enjoyed himself at Janis's Ph.D. graduation c

By the time Saul reached seventy, the man he had be his teens and his late forties so filled my father wit shame that he felt a need to alter, repudiate, an deny that past while he still could do so. Saul and he forgave little in himself. Plagued by se]

came from astronomically high standards, my father was acutely aware of what he had done and not done. At the same time Saul hated admitting that he was wrong or even had once been so. Revisions of such magnitude forced Saul to call upon and often blend his mental and verbal agility; his ability to compartmentalize his life; his firm inner division between life and art; and his propensity to avoid introspection.

But his past was my past, and the years he wanted to bury were filled for me with pleasant memories and people I loved. I looked back on them with fondness, but Saul's nostalgia was highly selective. Distancing himself from "young Saul" drove yet another wedge between me and the young father I loved and wanted to preserve. Though I had established a life in California apart from him, revisions of his personal history compounded the reversals of his socio-cultural beliefs and became new hot spots in a long cold war that further eroded our already tenuous common ground.

"Young Saul's" questioning of authority had encompassed rebellion against his father, political radicalism, and departure from his Jewish roots; these were formative components of my own ethos. Becoming a famous writer and the literary persona he cultivated came, for reasons I cannot fully understand, to necessitate repudiating his youthful questioning and demeaning people toward whom I felt loyal. When he went too far, I disinterred what he was trying to bury, which infuriated him because he knew I had a historical point.

But independence was not a simple matter for either of us. I felt conflicted because I loved and I wanted to please him. Saul, too, was limited because he could not allow himself to mimic Abraham's overt demands for filial compliance, yet he desired

just that from his own sons. Instead, Saul used a number of subtler forms of direct and indirect pressure on me and family members, often calling upon "family feeling," a relic of communal sacrifice left over from Lachine, to get his way with us.

The choice of a single financial adviser for several family members illustrates Saul's pressure to conform with his wishes irrespective of our needs. During the 1980s, Saul used Jeff Krol as an accountant and was pleased with his work and his investment advice. Soon he urged Lesha, Aunt Jane, and me to follow suit and use him. I resisted for several years, but I had a growing interest in my own finances and had made a small investment in Sam and Shael's chain of nursing homes in Chicago, which made Jeff's location appealing. Saul was delighted when I switched, and matters went along smoothly for a few years until he reversed course, unceremoniously ended his relationship with Jeff, and expected me to follow suit immediately. I was happy with Jeff's work and refused, but had to endure several years of my father's direct pressure to stop using him. Eventually, I moved back to my California accountant. Saul was greatly pleased, but even that did not stop him from complaining about how long I had taken to follow his wishes. This was just one of many episodes contributing to my fatigue with the overused phrase *family feeling*, which lost its power to sway me after I realized Saul's demands for loyalty translated as following his current whim and expecting sacrifices that vastly outnumbered any he made for me or my family.

Among the beliefs Saul distanced himself from were Reichianism and the hedonistic behavior it had helped him to rationalize. In the 1950s, however, he had been in dead earnest. After sitting in Isaac Rosenfeld's orgone box, before he built his own, Saul told Arthur Lidov that a wart on one of his fingers had disappeared. When Arthur scoffed, Saul withdrew, hurt. Arthur's widow recently told me that it was not long after this incident that their friendship ended, an ending Arthur attributed to his open skepticism about Reich.

A glimmer of shame over his personal selfishness and the harm he had inflicted on Anita occurred during my visit with Saul and Janis during an academic quarter they spent in Paris. He and I took long walks around town, during which he pointed out places where we had lived. On a Paris street he confessed to being plagued by guilt toward Anita, saying, "I can't go around a corner without seeing a reminder of your mother and the pain I caused her."

Shame was part of Saul's reason for protecting me from his philandering, but that comment in Paris was the only time he mentioned it. And I only brought it up once after becoming upset by a sexual liaison reported in James Atlas's biography. When I asked Saul about it, he denied the event, derided Atlas, and asked if there was anything else I wanted to know about the past. I demurred. Later I felt I had let Anita's memory down by not telling him how angry I was whenever I thought about the unhappiness his chronic infidelity had caused her.

Saul had become disillusioned long before with the kind of doctrinaire rigidity that compelled the Trotskyite Oscar Tarcov to end his romance with a Stalinist girlfriend. In a scene from *Dangling Man*, written in 1944, Joseph is outraged when a former comrade he encounters in a restaurant will not even say hello. Saul saw the Marxist beliefs that had fueled his philandering, bohemianism, and permissive parenting as shameful errors and minimized them. Saul's rebellion against his father had included refusing to go into the coal business, pursuing a career as a writer, arguing about politics and money, and flaunting his rejection of Abraham's adherence to Jewish customs. Saul eventually stopped mentioning his arguments with Abraham altogether and came to speak about Grandpa with a fondness that surprised me. Perhaps because they had had so many bitter confrontations, he tried not to argue with me. Trying to avoid his tirades, I usually did the same, although I was always troubled by his revised versions of family life that omitted his painful relationship with his father.

I have no doubt Saul came to rue the freedom he and Anita had given me, perhaps because the independence it nurtured drew me away from him and made me resistant to the influence he belatedly tried to assert. Occasional bitter disagreements emerged when I rejected a return to a world, or a family, held together by the accumulated wisdom of previous generations as defined by my father. Generational conflicts grounded in his assumption of the kind of authority he had formerly rejected now largely replaced our differences over cultural politics.

Of all of Saul's revisions of the life he had led, none was more startling than a comment he made about five years before his death. On a walk in Boston, he volunteered out of the blue, "I should never have divorced your mother." Flabbergasted, I expressed my doubt that he could have written his novels without divorcing Anita and pursuing the more independent life of a writer. He brushed my objections off, as if he could have written *Herzog*, a book filled with the misery of his second failed marriage, anyway. I can only conclude that Saul never forgave himself for leaving us.

That comment and another he made late in life touched

directly upon the way he wrote about himself and about people in his life, and, by extension, on the ways he separated art and life. I visited Saul in Boston, deeply troubled by a recent ethical violation by a colleague. I brought up my concern over the frightening power of therapists to shape the lives of their patients. My father's response was that he'd never want to be married to any of his women characters. I was speechless at how he could see no resemblance between his wives and the women married to his narrators, but he genuinely felt that he had created his characters entirely from imagination. When asked about his characters, Saul always maintained that he gave them the traits he deemed necessary to make a larger literary point.

On the other hand, Saul certainly wrote in the heat of anger after his second and third divorces. And, to the chagrin of many, his published works gave him the last word. Ex-wives, failed reality instructors, and "disloyal" friends were irritated and hurt but defenseless as Saul pinpointed their eccentricities and cataloged their wrongs. And I will confess to breathing easier after finishing each novel without, as far as I know, being the object of his scorn. But I remain convinced that his novels were not simply or even primarily written to get even with those who hurt him because, were that the case, Saul Bellow would never have become the great writer that he was.

That is not to say that Saul's firm line between life and art is not open to serious question. He crossed it freely in novel after novel while attacking anyone who asserted that he had done so. Such literary license can and often does bleed into blatant thievery. And stealing someone's personhood is not a victimless crime. To the contrary, it is a crime whose victims simply have no voice. It is not—as I recently heard Benjamin Taylor, editor of my father's recently published letters, assert—an honor to be immortalized in a great work of art.

Though not at my father's hands, I was a minor victim who can testify. Philip Roth's *Everyman* contains a funeral scene reminiscent of Saul's during which a fictional character speaks, almost verbatim, my final graveside words to my father as I tossed a ceremonial handful of dirt onto Saul's coffin. I was barely grazed in this literary skirmish but felt ill-used enough to better understand that people I care about were hurt by my father's books. Edith Tarcov, feeling overly exposed by a loving portrait in *Mr. Sammler's Planet*, did not want to go out in public for a year after the novel was published. Even Jack Ludwig, who openly spoke about being the model for Valentine Gersbach in *Herzog*, has, I've been told, changed his tune since becoming a grandfather. And I can barely imagine the effects on Sasha, Susan, and Alexandra of being pilloried in a novel and having no defense.

No aspect of Saul's past conduct became more shameful to him than having distanced himself from his Jewish roots for over thirty years out of Marxist conviction, as a part of his literary apprenticeship he considered necessary, and because organized religious observance so little moved him. During those years he resisted the label of "Jewish writer," once pointedly declaring that he liked hockey, but no critic labeled him a Blackhawk fan. And he had allowed me to decide not to go to Hebrew school without uttering a word for three decades.

The time Saul spent in Israel during the 1967 war touched something deep within and, no doubt, made him feel ashamed of having blinded himself to the full impact of the horrors of the Holocaust and to his departure from Jewish self-identification. As an older man and an established author, he reversed himself and publicly embraced being a Jewish writer. He signed petitions in support of Israel and offered his support to writers who had suffered from anti-Semitism in the Soviet Union.

He also covered over his personal rejection of Jewish customs. It was during the years when he was busily revising his past that my aunt Marge told me the story about Grandpa Abraham's horror at finding a ham in Saul and Anita's icebox. When I relayed the amusing story to an eighty-five-year-old Saul, he vehemently denied it. But knowing my parents' attitudes, the details Marge had provided, and a plethora of stories told by other family members—like Saul borrowing Sam's car to visit his friends on Yom Kippur—I tend to believe her.

Saul never admitted to being ashamed of having let me choose not to have a bar mitzvah, but by the mid-1980s he must have concluded that he had erred decades earlier. His change of heart and the pressure he exerted boiled down generational disagreements into a battle over how to raise a child who knows right from wrong. As my son approached his teens, Saul began to urge me to force Andrew to attend Hebrew school and have a bar mitzvah. He began by chiding me about ignorance of my religious heritage, a charge that I readily admitted as true but that also sidestepped an argument. Dissatisfied with his failure to change my attitudes or behavior vis-à-vis my son, he ratcheted up the pressure by telling me how important it was that Andrew should learn about his heritage (although he never made any mention of Juliet's need for a Jewish education).

In the face of direct pressure from Saul I remained unwilling to force my son to go through a public ritual that I considered empty. I became convinced that his reversal after years of silence was an attempt to make up for his own departure from his Jewish roots. When he persevered, I countered his arguments about the virtue of religious training by cataloging the moral failures of observant men and maintaining that faith was too often the last refuge of scoundrels. When even that failed to silence Saul, I reminded him of his acquiescence in my lack of Jewish education and he backed off.

Finally Saul stopped lobbying me directly, but as often happened when he remained displeased, a messenger soon arrived in the person of Ruth Wisse, a Harvard scholar of Yiddish who had befriended Saul and Janis in Boston. I had not met Ruth, but he told me how much he loved speaking Yiddish with her. Ruth attended a conference at Stanford, and I was invited to a reception where she introduced herself. I was glad to meet a friend of Saul's until, after exchanging a few pleasantries, she began to badger me about Andrew's bar mitzvah. I don't know whether Ruth had taken it upon herself to deliver Saul's message or whether he had charged her to do so. In either case, it was apparent that Ruth knew about the details of a conflict I considered a private family matter.

Still angry on my next trip to Boston, I triggered a final brutal argument about Andrew's religious training when I refused to let our long-standing joke about Michael Riff's religious confusion pass for humor. I accused Morris Riff, the atheist father of my childhood friend, of being a hypocrite because he forced his son to have a bar mitzvah. "You don't teach your child about good and evil by saying one thing and doing another," I told Saul, who went ballistic. He said that

Michael's father, whom he had never met, was a poor immigrant father trying to cling to his traditions in a new world. As Janis wisely told both of us to knock it off, I realized that Saul saw his own immigrant father in Morris Riff and that I was calling my father and grandfather hypocrites for insisting on the ritual. Incidentally, Michael ended up as a fine scholar of twentieth-century Jewish history.

Even before Saul became famous, people told me they did not know how to approach him, whether to do so at all, or what to say. Now, after being fed by decades of celebrity, the awe in which people held my father made what he said about his past incontrovertible. His fame fostered a literary persona that Saul fueled by saying he was born to write. When someone asked if he had considered another career, his clever answer was to ask whether they would pose the same question to an earthworm. Saul also fostered the notion that academia had offered him little in his development as a writer and that he was largely self-taught. Saul's characterization of his first two novels as his M.A. and Ph.D. is meant to portray a young writer patterning himself after the European masters, but he omits that the novels were partly tailored to prove his worth to anti-Semitic academicians.

    I fully agree that the academic study of literature offered little to him as a writer, but by cultivating a literary persona that included the notion that he was tutored only by the great writers, Saul ignored the support and criticism he received from friends, colleagues, family, and even strangers. Saul revered Isaac Rosenfeld and, no doubt, profited from his friend's prescient judgments and criticism as well as from others with whom "young Saul" eagerly shared work in progress. He read aloud to visitors in our home, but I have no recollection of his doing that in his later years.

According to Mitzi McClosky, Saul bristled when Robert Penn Warren praised *The Victim* but also noted its linear form, which disappeared in Saul's next novel, *The Adventures of Augie March*. And I witnessed a similar moment when we met Robert Frost. I was ten and Saul had brought me to his reading in the Bard College gym. All I remember is Frost's flowing white hair, but an intrepid Saul introduced himself to the poet, saying he had "come down from New York" to hear him. Frost brought him up short by saying, "You mean up from New York." No doubt stung, Saul often repeated the story without comment. But I now realize that he also took to heart Frost's tacit lesson that every word counts.

I was most troubled by the ways he revised the personal side of his early career. His late-life version went beyond minimizing the support he got to including chronic harsh criticism of those he knew had helped him. Although Anita had urged Saul to take a year off from work to write while she supported them and offered emotional support when his self-confidence wavered, he buried the respect in which he had once openly held my mother. He said nothing about her support, irritating both her and me. His private revision extended to my daughter, Juliet, who was twelve when her grandmother died. When, as a graduate student, she asked Saul to tell her about Anita, all he could muster from a fifteen-year marriage was the disappointing answer that she was a good dancer. As if that were not enough, Saul felt it necessary to go on the offensive, complaining about how my grandmother Goshkin's control emasculated her sons. Over and over he scoffed at the cultural shortcomings of the Goshkins and derided Beebee's romantic frivolity.

I was angered by these personal attacks because Beebee, Edith Tarcov, and my aging Goshkin aunts were very important to me and still alive. By the 1980s they all lived in New York and looked out for one another. My brothers and former stepmothers had also moved to New York. Sasha had remarried happily. Susan, who never remarried, lived nearby too. These two little groups made up the East Coast branch of my family, and I visited at least once a year.

Edith Tarcov, by then widowed, lived in a tiny apartment across the street from my aunts, and Saul continued to visit her regularly. Edith, who never really recognized my parents' divorce, kept him apprised of the welfare of his "sisters-in-law," as she called Anita's sisters Catherine and Ida, and arranged for Saul to join them for a cup of tea, steeped, of course, in the old Russian fashion. Catherine took advantage of his visit to exact her revenge for Abraham's snub almost fifty years earlier, when he had left a family lunch to take a nap; she noted that Saul "had certainly come a long way in life, considering . . ." Her meaning was not lost on Saul, who was wounded when reminded of that infamous postwedding lunch and the Goshkins's judgment of his family as lowly and ill-mannered.

Several years later, my aunts joined my family for a week on Cape Cod. Catherine died soon after returning to New York. Ida, now living alone, thought that Edith Tarcov would outlive her and be a source of support. But Edith had poor lungs. When Beebee's daily call was not returned, she let herself into Edith's apartment to find that she had died alone. After the police came to Edith's apartment, Beebee was unwilling to leave her body until one of Edith's children came. The officer told Beebee that the apartment had to be sealed for several days after the coroner removed the body. Beebee was concerned about Edith's beloved African violets. "Who will water them?" she asked. The officer responded, "Get real, lady." When I told Saul the story about Edith's flowers, he went into his usual diatribe that Beebee was a "fey girl" who paid little attention to the real world. I countered in irritation that Beebee had always been devoted to me and, long ago, had been equally devoted to Saul and Anita. As far as I was concerned, I went on, Beebee was the woman who scoured New York markets to find fresh strawberries because she knew how I loved them and wanted to make sure they were available for my early-spring birthday celebrations. I never heard another bad word from him about her and wished I'd spoken up earlier.

After the deaths of Edith Tarcov and Ida Goshkin, Beebee began to suffer from a brain syndrome that caused a rapid deterioration in memory. Soon she had to have full-time care, and she died a few years later. When I called to tell Saul she had died, we shared a moment of deep sorrow, and he was pleased when I sent him a copy of the tribute I wrote, which her nephew read at her memorial service.

About ten years before his death, in a rare semiconfessional moment, Saul mused aloud about his family. The Bellow family contained, he said, a sadist (Morrie), a masochist (Sam) . . . Fascinated, I moved to the edge of my chair in anticipation of what he might say about himself, but his voice trailed off. I knew what should have come next, but he was unwilling to address his self-preoccupation or that of his sister.

Saul's novels contain occasional refreshing outbursts of honest regret that contrast with the revisionism about the past that filled our conversations. Artur Sammler's admission of having blinded himself to his true history by turning away from his Jewish roots is the most genuine of these novelistic confessions, since Saul actually did return to his Jewish roots after covering the 1967 war. In *The Dean's December*, published ten years after his 1977 Jefferson Lectures, Saul's narrator, Albert Corde, has long conversations with a high school friend and rival, Dewey Spangler. Spangler has become a journalist and a man of the world, while Corde seems to have drifted during a career that has culminated in his deanship. When Corde publishes two controversial articles laying out a dark vision of American life, generating a storm of protest, Spangler, a man all too familiar with both the pitfalls of writing about public matters and Corde's youthful idealism, chastises his old friend for the obvious misstep of writing so boldly about public issues. In Spangler's criticisms I see my father chastising himself for falling victim to the seductions of fame by making pronouncements in his Jefferson Lectures that went well beyond literature.

Charlie Citrine's inability to rid himself of the contamination caused by the pleasures of fame and fortune closely parallels my father's disappointment with himself and disillusionment with the teachings of Rudolf Steiner. But Saul's curiosity about an afterlife and his quest for a path to immortality never stopped. In *More Die of Heartbreak*, Saul lodges in Kenneth Trachtenberg a deep knowledge of mysticism that may have paralleled Saul's continued reading post-Steiner. And at moments Saul certainly appeared to have transferred his concerns from this world to the next. At a lecture in San Francisco, Saul gave near the end of his life, he responded to an audience question about what happens after death with "It's the only *real* question." To me that comment dismissed equally important questions about living in this world, on which Saul appeared to have given up. And, in that light, I was not surprised when told that a well-worn copy of the New Testament was on Saul's bedside table during his final illness.

But moments of self-doubt, tacit apologies, and even admissions of error by Saul's narrators are not equally genuine, as his backward-looking novella, *The Actual*, reveals. Harry Trellman appears to be reconsidering his rootless life when he makes a proposal of marriage to his high school sweetheart, Amy Wustrin. He now insists that the sincerity of his love for her was genuine, even though in high school his life direction was already firmly set in his mind. But Amy, who knows better, challenges Harry, saying he was much more interested in high-flown philosophical ideas than he was in her.

And so, I believe, was Saul, who chose a life of singular literary purpose and a lifelong pattern of selfish conduct that he could neither deny nor completely bury. I fought his revisionism and held tightly to pleasant memories, but only later did I realize that I did so because I was far closer to Saul as a child than I was as an adult. Saul recognized the ill effects of the distance between us more clearly than I. He sent me the photo that became the dust jacket of this memoir inscribed on the back with words about father-son closeness, which for us was sadly long past. I keep that photo before me as I write, even today.

If burying our past were not enough, our relationship was further strained by my father's discomfort and notable lack of interest in the priorities I gave to my family and my career as a psychotherapist. Saul's disinclination to introspection, no doubt something he considered a way to protect his creativity, always made him wary of my career. Saul maintained, with considerable pride, that he had decided to ignore his psychological problems. Long ago he had put his faith in willpower. Anita told me that Saul had overcome his extreme ticklishness by simply deciding to stop. As a child I often tested him and, sure enough, he never flinched when I tickled him. During our Paris years, Saul stopped smoking his pipe overnight when sores in his mouth were diagnosed as precancerous.

But a purposeful rejection of his personal weaknesses explained only in part his skeptical attitude toward what can be learned from looking inward to explain one's motivations and behavior. He felt that neither of his therapies had been very helpful, and perhaps believed the opposite. He was taken with Wilhelm Reich's ideas about emotion, but was never convinced by Reich's foolish late-life ideas about orgone energy. Later however, Saul told Barley Alison, his British publisher, that Reichianism had precipitated his divorcing my mother. His analysis with the cerebral Dr. Meehl could only have compounded his suspicions about insights gained from therapeutic introspection. Saul ridiculed psychiatric overuse of interpretation in his novella *A Theft*. And, no doubt, he found Freud's boiling down creativity to the sublimation of libido an offensive notion.

I found that psychoanalytic theory best encompassed the complexity I knew was also central to Saul's view of man and thought an appreciation of the mysteries of human nature was central to the common ground between us. After positive experiences as a patient, unlike Saul's, I found introspection to be a valuable form of facing emotional truth, for my patients and for myself. I came to see the unconscious as a personal asset and an ally in my work, but it made Saul uneasy. He was interested in a psychology that explained behavior that was contradictory or mysterious only if it contained a comprehensible logical thread. Once, Saul was puzzled when a friend's marriage fell apart after the death of an adult child under suspicious circumstances. In a rare exception at odds with his usual lack of interest, he asked me why the parents were acting so savagely toward one another. I explained that, in their grief, they could not afford to blame the child and took their anger out on each other. Satisfied with an explanation that melded the inner life with rationality, Saul thanked me without further comment.

Saul's antipsychoanalytic views softened a bit after he read the book I gave him by Heinz Kohut, whom he had consulted briefly at Susan's insistence as their marriage deteriorated. Kohut's theories on the self were an alternate psychoanalytic theory I found sufficiently appealing to make it the subject of my doctoral thesis. His ideas appealed to Saul and became part of our debate about the differences between a "human soul," which included a spiritual dimension, and an "inner self" I limited to the secular realm.

I have wondered if Saul's dislike of my career stemmed from a fear that I could see through the barriers he took such pains to cultivate with everyone. Perhaps on some level he anticipated that I'd use my understanding of him in a public account. No matter the causes of our disagreements about psychoanalysis, we simply stopped discussing the value of introspection.

I was unhappy about Saul's distance from my family. He

never got along with my wife after she refused to listen to his complaints about me. Though he expressed excitement about becoming a grandfather, Saul showed little desire to spend time with Juliet or Andrew on our visits to Chicago, where all of the grandparents lived, unless I accompanied them. His trips to California were not to visit me or my family per se. He usually arranged to deliver a lecture or attend a large public event in his honor and then tacked on a few days with us, during which he complained about not receiving the same kind of grand receptions from us that he got from his lecture hosts.

Neither of my children grew close to their grandfather, and in acknowledgment of his scant attention, I told them when each turned eighteen that their relationships with Saul were in their hands. Juliet had hurt her grandfather's feelings by choosing Columbia over the University of Chicago, but when Saul and Janis moved to Boston, Juliet, encouraged by her uncle Adam, traveled there several times in hopes of cultivating her own relationship with Saul. These visits were often unpleasant for Juliet, as Saul vacillated between complaining about family members and peppering her with questions about Andrew's lack of interest in academic subjects. When she began to date Charlie Schulman, her future husband and a longtime friend of my brother Dan's, Saul took to grilling both Juliet and Charlie about Dan's welfare rather than expressing interest in their lives.

I knew how engaging Saul was and how much fun he could be with children. I had hoped the attention he lavished on me as a child would extend to my children, and while I was not thinking about it consciously, perhaps I hoped that the closeness that had waned between us would be revived through

Juliet and Andrew. I was never sure if his reticence was a sign of resentment that my energies were not directed toward him or a reflection of his own fatigue with parenthood after raising three sons.

With our relationship at its lowest point, I took to visiting Saul in Boston by myself. Occasionally our emotional bond would reassert itself spontaneously. I was a mediocre student in college, but when I received my doctorate in clinical social work in 1981, Saul, on a visit to California, was moved to tears and said, "My Herschele [a diminutive of my Yiddish name] got a Ph.D."

More often than not, however, I had to make deliberate efforts to keep our tattered connection alive. Saul loved to build fires, and even in summer he took the chill off the Vermont mornings with a bright little blaze. As he aged, I began to think of my efforts to reestablish a now-elusive closeness as stirring up fireplace embers that grew dimmer every year as we fondly remembered a familiar cast of characters from both sides of the family and a long list of friends.

During the first years of their marriage, Janis was friendly toward Saul's sons. She asked after our children and correctly took no maternal role with me, as I was about fifteen years her senior. Certainly Janis owed us no debt, and perhaps she was put off by our initial resistance to their marriage. But there was a level of restraint that had been absent in my relationships with Sasha, Susan, and Alexandra, who made efforts to get to know me apart from my tie to Saul. Sasha and I had grown close. Susan was pleasant to me, and Alexandra acted as another grandmother to Juliet.

All three sons were used to our father remarrying. We lived with different mothers and had custody arrangements that resulted in rarely having to share Saul with one another. I was thirteen when Adam was born and in college when Dan arrived, circumstances that muted sibling rivalry. We each had time alone with Saul, who found ways to show his love for all three sons. Now grown, we were more than willing to cede Janis the primacy in Saul's affections she appeared to desire. But I believe she misunderstood that we had become used to sharing his love with each other and with each new wife. Janis also seemed not to understand that all three sons were used to taking his chronic complaining about us when irritated in stride—knowing it would soon blow over.

During Saul and Janis's first years together, they traveled to a number of public events in the United States, Europe, and Israel. They moved to Boston to be nearer the recently completed Vermont house, where old friends like Vicki Lidov Fishman and Zita Cogan and new ones like Stanley Crouch and Martin Amis visited. Now that Saul and Alexandra were divorced, Allan Bloom was once again a welcome figure in Saul's home.

When you are as different from your fellow men as Saul, it is natural to be drawn to someone like Allan Bloom, with whom he shared personal, intellectual, and political views. Allan's deep knowledge of Plato's ideas about the soul, his study of Romanticism, and his inveterate matchmaking sufficiently endeared him to Saul that my father overcame a lifelong aversion to homosexuals and even added Allan to his long chain of reality instructors. My visits with Saul became less frequent during these years, and I never met Allan, but his influence loomed large. Saul's last work, *Ravelstein*, is a magnificent memoir of Bloom, barely disguised as a novel, so filled with actual events, feelings Saul shared, and matters the entire family spoke about that I take the book as largely a work of nonfiction.

Bloom and Saul taught courses together on Flaubert and Stendhal, whose romantic novels revolve around characters who extend themselves to achieve capacities they once only imagined. Allan illuminated these expansive notions with discussions of the power of Eros and Plato's explanation of the yearning between the sexes. According to Plato, men and women were once physically united and their long-lost union underlies their mutual attraction.

The ability to move beyond one's personal limitations and the attraction between man and woman merge into what I call Bloom's love formula: the plausible rationale he offered Saul when his optimism about love was at its lowest. As Saul's marriage to Alexandra was failing, Allan challenged his friend to overcome his misgivings and to try love once more. Janis was also captivated by Allan's ideas about the transformative power of love and by the idea that there is a perfect match out there waiting to be made. Surely, such a bright, well-educated woman needed a reason to justify marriage to a man who would leave her childless and a young widow. And that reason, the truest love for Saul, swept away fears of her future.

At seventy and recently divorced for the fourth time, it is no wonder that my father was cautious about love. Saul wanted to look carefully before leaping into another marriage, especially one so tinged by imbalances that his self-interest was too transparent to deny. I expected that my father, after following so much bad advice over a lifetime, would have been able to kick

the reality instructor habit. But, like his advice-giving prede-
cessors, Bloom sounded as if he knew what he was talking about.
His advice about love was good enough for Saul to put his faith
in a gay man dying of AIDS. Ignoring a lifetime of lambasting
similar romantic notions he decried in Beebee, my father
opted to let Bloom ply his philosophical wares and followed his
advice because it offered a rationale to divorce Alexandra and
marry Janis.

Bloom's theories are manifest in the wisdom of Abe Ravelstein, the novel's title character, who has it all figured out—
history, politics, philosophy, money, and the relationship
between the sexes, to mention a few subjects. Why shouldn't
Chick, the novel's pseudo naive narrator, allow Abe to instruct
him in matters of love? After all, Abe has already made an assessment of Chick's problem with women: what he calls
Chick's nihilism is insufficient to allow him to recognize and
accept the love Rosamund feels for him. Abe thinks that Chick
is so constrained by knots of conventional morality that he cannot take the necessary, though self-interested, steps that would
make him happy, dumping his wife, Vela, for Rosamund. Abe
argues that Vela is insufficiently feminine. There is no cooking,
no loving, too much independence, and not enough warmth in
the marriage. Abe thinks it's no wonder Chick's soul is in a
state of need. Furthermore, Abe will have none of his friend's
self-denial and urges Chick to say to himself, "To hell with
convention. The woman loves you. Go for it."

Saul's two dearest friends, Isaac Rosenfeld and Allan Bloom—
the men who understood him most fully, represented by two
literary characters—make an identical and wholly accurate assess-

ment of my father. Isaac as King Dafu and Allan as Abe Ravelstein realize that their complementary characters, Gene Henderson and Chick, both suffer from an inability to give and take love freely. I believe that to have been Saul's greatest personal flaw, and through the mouths of Dafu and Abe, my father seems to agree.

Saul demanded more from family than he gave. As witness to all of his marriages, I saw that my mother, her successors, and all three sons expected more attention and emotional support than my father could provide. Our hard edges were rightly sharpened by disappointment, but Saul could give no more.

However, Allan Bloom's formula fueled a genuine love and a long marriage between Saul and Janis. Despite my initial reservations, their relationship stands apart. There is no doubt that she broke through the icy cold to which Saul had resigned himself after his marriage to Alexandra failed. And, I would add, Janis is unique in maintaining that she does not suffer from the disappointments other family members feel.

I have concluded that Saul's observation about love in *Ravelstein* holds the key. Matters of the heart should not to be second-guessed by "objective" outsiders, including myself, who thought Janis's love was overly selfless. As far as my father was concerned, her love was "just the ticket," as he used to say when highly pleased.

Chapter Ten

SAUL IN DECLINE: 1994–2005

SAUL ALMOST DIED during the Thanksgiving weekend of 1994. A winter trip to the Caribbean intended to cheer my father, who was still grieving Allan Bloom's 1992 death, went totally wrong. Saul's fictionalized account in *Ravelstein* closely matches the whirlwind chain of events as I understand them: a warm swim, a toxic fish at dinner, confusion over a man who was very sick, a flight to Boston, an ambulance ride to the emergency room, more confusion, and a life almost lost several times during his first night in the hospital. Dan, Adam, and I soon joined Janis in Boston. Saul's diagnosis remained uncertain and he lay in a medically induced coma as day after day passed and we sat in his hospital room, analyzing each new tidbit of medical news. Janis, saying that Saul would want a full report when he awoke, took notes on a large yellow pad.

All but the most pressing practical considerations were blotted out. Our tiny world was like a series of concentric circles that surrounded and protected him. In the innermost ring was Saul, protected by Janis. She was in a complete state of exhaustion after staying up for days, and her health worried the nurses and the three of us. But Janis refused to go home, claiming she needed nothing but a toothbrush and a few clean T-shirts. The next ring held Dan, Adam, and me; we agreed our primary job was to protect Janis and Saul. Once the news of his illness got out, that job expanded to keeping people who were worried about him informed but at bay. Lesha wanted to come to Boston but agreed to settle for phone calls several times a day. She, in turn, kept the rest of the Bellow family up-to-date.

The ring beyond immediate family included his agent, Harriet Wasserman, his lawyer, his friends, and his colleagues. Harriet, who had recently recovered from her own serious medical problems, was convinced that only the doctor who had saved her life could save Saul's. She pressed to come to Boston even before I got there, but Adam and I knew Harriet's meddling would upset Janis. We tried to keep her occupied with a chore: securing some ready cash for Janis, who, it turned out, did not have access to Saul's bank accounts. But Harriet soon started hounding me again and would not agree to stay in New York until I lost my temper and she relented.

As I sat by Saul's bedside on what would have been Anita's eightieth birthday, Janis played a CD of Handel's *Water Music*, a composition that always reminded me of the good times during my childhood. I burst into tears and ran out of the room as the impact of having lost one parent and the possibility that I'd lose the other hit me. When I returned I explained my tears to a sympathetic Janis. While Saul was still in a coma, another loss occurred. I received a call from my wife telling me that George Sarant, Isaac Rosenfeld's son, had died of a fatal heart attack, much like the one that had killed Isaac almost forty years earlier. With my emotions already worn thin, I could not remain sitting in a hospital room. I needed a break and went to New

York, where my daughter, Juliet, then a college student, and Beebee sustained me for several days. I made sure that my visit allowed me to attend the memorial service for George. After Saul's failure to attend Isaac's or Oscar Tarcov's funeral, I was determined to ensure a Bellow was present this time.

Janis and I talked about how to tell my father, knowing that the news of George's death would devastate Saul, who would awaken frail and weakened. I needed to hold off telling him until Janis told me Saul was strong enough to tolerate such a blow. But about two weeks after my return to California, I became concerned that one of his visitors would let slip that George had died. After consulting with Janis, I called to deliver the awful news. In one of our most painful yet binding moments, tears flowed on both ends of the phone after Saul's wail of pain as he learned that Isaac's son had died just like his father had.

As Saul was about to be wakened from his induced coma, Janis made it clear that she was in charge and, despite appearances, had the strength for the job. After two weeks of sitting in his hospital room, hanging on every medical detail, sharing concern for Saul's welfare, and cooperating in the plan to tell Saul that George Sarant had died, I had no reason not to trust Janis. I told her that I had no wish to be burdened with his physical care or to make decisions. Silently I thought that a man who had left three sons in the custody of their mothers could not expect to call on those sons to care for his day-to-day welfare. And my conversations with Saul about Alexandra's inability to take care of him and about the sacrifices Janis would make by marrying him showed how well he understood the need to bank on someone other than us during the years when he feared, correctly, he would be in decline.

I ardently hoped that nearly dying would change Saul into a man glad to be alive and desirous of improving our tattered relationship. Not so. After several months dominated by reports of Saul's returning strength, Lesha visited with him in Vermont. With Janis sitting quietly by, Saul, in a rage at his sons, told her that while he was in a coma, Adam, Dan, and I expressed a desire for our father to die so that we could inherit his estate. Lesha shot back, "That's ridiculous, the boys came to Boston to help." Further angered, Saul challenged Lesha to check it out for herself if she didn't believe him. Shocked and frightened by the damage that could result, Lesha called me. Angry about a report I knew to be false, I grudgingly repeated the entire chronology that I had relayed to her over the phone from Boston while Saul was in a coma.

Lesha and I speculated whether Janis could be the source of Saul's information. No one but she and his three sons were present. And Janis had taken notes throughout those days because, she said, Saul would want to be fully informed when he awakened. As well, both of us knew that touching on filial greed and parricidal wishes elicited the most powerful of forces in the Bellow family—the specter of Abraham's chronic threats to disinherit his children, along with images of King Lear and the hated father Karamazov.

I never questioned Janis's love or devotion to Saul. However, I have come to believe that after caring for a husband in a weakened condition for six months and the prospect of having to do so perhaps for years, Allan Bloom's notions about making sacrifices purely for love no longer proved a sufficient rationale. Based on a series of actions taken over the next months and years that, in my mind, amounted to a coup d'état, I can only presume Janis had come to feel a need to go beyond ensuring her primacy in Saul's affections to exert a level of control that expanded well past his daily life to include financial, legal, and literary decision making. Her actions could have easily driven a powerful wedge between Saul and his sons, but had the opposite effect on my father and me.

I did not mind honoring Janis's authority by fading further into the background than I already had. What I did mind was being demonized when my brothers and I had tried to protect Janis and our father while both were so vulnerable. I remained incensed at his accusation of malice and greed which followed on the heels of what appeared to be Janis's friendliness and cooperation, and my accession to her status as Saul's caretaker.

Eighteen months later, when Saul had recovered most of his strength, I visited him in Boston determined to clear the air. I said that I wanted to speak with him about what had transpired during his illness. Saul interrupted with an apology for not remembering that I was in Boston while he was in a coma. "Hard as I've tried, I can't remember a thing, and everything I know about what happened comes from Janis." I told Saul I didn't expect him to remember me but continued by asking whether he believed I was "sitting around in the hospital waiting for him to die so I could get my hands on some dough." "No, we don't have that kind of relationship" was his immediate response. My father was alluding to my thirty years of financial independence, which had spared us the arguments over money that had so plagued the other branches of the Bellow family.

My question whetted Saul's curiosity, as the rumors about Janis's state of mind must have reached him. In response to his question, I described the concentric circles around them and how Janis had protected Saul for days on end with little sleep and eating almost nothing. I continued, "Lord knows what she went through, but it must have been hell. In a crisis like that everyone is affected, but I've learned never to draw any permanent connotations from how people act when under duress." Saul, in his usual response to having received a satisfactory explanation, was silent.

A decade later, Zachary Leader, a new biographer for Saul who had been selected by Janis, shed a clearer light on her behavior toward me and Lesha during and after Saul's illness. According to Leader, a biographical source had told him that Lesha and I had hatched a secret plan to declare Janis legally incompetent, strip her of her control over Saul, and take him to Cincinnati to be near his sister, Jane. Leader asked Adam and Dan about the plan. Of course they knew nothing of a nonexistent plan to disenfranchise Janis and essentially kidnap Saul. Until that point, I had not been willing to discuss my father with Leader, but my brothers were so distressed by his questions that they insisted I speak freely with the biographer about the matter. After denying a story about events that were never contemplated, let alone discussed, I asked Leader about his source for such a wild idea. He refused to identify the person other than assuring me that it was not Janis. I took the opportunity to caution Mr. Leader about the credibility of anyone who would spread such a story without evidence and added that my brothers and I had been similarly maligned and remained sensitive.

Such a ridiculous story reveals what extreme concern there must have been about the influence of Saul's family. And,

ironically, a form of "kidnapping" akin to what Lesha and I
had been accused of did occur. Over the next five years, Janis
gradually broadened her control over every aspect of my father's life. She spoke for him and, at times, substituted her own
desires for those I believed to have been his. Soon Saul was
represented by a new literary agent, a new lawyer, and new financial advisers. In the end Janis was installed as Saul's literary
executor, a new will was drafted, Lesha was removed as executor/
trustee, and the inheritance Adam, Dan, and I were told to expect was, at a minimum, halved. We were excluded from any
posthumous financial benefit from Saul's literary estate. And the
changes did not stop at financial and legal control. Eventually
Janis was to become a mother and, most symbolically, to have
the final say over where Saul would be buried.

Harriet Wasserman, Saul's literary agent for more than twenty-
five years and a daily presence in his life, was first to go. New
literary agents were only too happy to court Saul Bellow. A
young man from the Wylie Agency arrived in Vermont while I
was visiting, quoting the poet Wordsworth at length, much to
my father's delight.

I cannot provide a better description of the end of Harriet's
tenure as Saul's agent than hers in *Handsome Is*, her memoir.
Harriet, who had delivered thousands of unpleasant messages
on Saul's behalf, knew how he hated delivering bad news in
person. Indirect hints were dropped and her power quickly
slipped away. Personnel from the Wylie Agency took over so
many of her responsibilities, it was obvious Saul had already
changed agents in all but name. Harriet rightly felt her years of
loyalty warranted that Saul should deliver the bad news himself, and she doggedly pushed for a personal resolution. Saul

kept putting her off, perhaps because he was not necessarily 100 percent in favor of firing her. Harriet waited for the inevitable call. When it finally came, she asked if Saul wanted her to fire herself, shielding him from one last unpleasant confrontation. The changing of the guard continued as Saul's lawyer, who had worked closely with Harriet, was replaced by Walter Pozen.

Janis nursed Saul back to health during two painful years of recuperation. By 1996, Saul had regained sufficient strength to attend Dan and Heather's wedding in Miami. In private, Saul informed Lesha of the legal and financial changes he had made. Outraged, particularly by their potential effects on his sons, she argued bitterly with her uncle behind closed doors. But Lesha was also loyal to Saul and gave us few indications of the radical changes he had authorized. Even in death, our father left the telling of bad news to the lawyers for his estate.

My first clear glimpse of a very personal change came by accident when, at their home on a visit in 1997 or '98, I took a phone message about an appointment for Janis from the fertility clinic at Boston's Brigham and Women's Hospital. I realized that Janis, and perhaps Saul, was intent on having a child. After telling Saul about the message, I expressed my surprise in light of our conversation during which he had disavowed having any more children. A clearly embarrassed Saul meekly said that he had asked Janis not to discuss the matter with him. I concluded that Janis was now intent on motherhood and Saul had no say other than asking her to keep the details to herself. Her desire to have a child was easy to understand, but at forty and with a husband over eighty, parenthood required a purposeful commitment. When that child, Rosie, arrived in 1999, her birth caused a stir inside and outside of the family. Saul gave multiple and contradictory versions of her conception. Knowing what steps Janis had taken, I found his differing accounts highly amusing. Saul enjoyed watching Rosie play and laugh. But when I visited my waning father, I was struck by the irony of a house occupied by a little creature so full of life and an old man who was rapidly declining and often bedridden.

The year 2000 saw two publications: my father's last novel, *Ravelstein*, and James Atlas's biography, *Bellow*. Writing *Ravelstein* was to be the proof that Saul Bellow had recovered his physical strength and his intellect. Saul's acknowledged portrait of Allan Bloom was generally well received, but he confirmed Allan's homosexuality publicly and identified AIDS as the likely cause of his death. In the minds of many political conservatives for whom Allan had become an intellectual mainstay after writing *The Closing of the American Mind*, publication of these personal details was an act of betrayal. Quickly Saul became embroiled in a firestorm that revealed his failing mental powers. He repeatedly told me that Allan had requested an honest portrait, and Saul reiterated that point to reporters until he realized the interviews he granted were only aggravating the controversy he had stirred up. Saul's memory and concentration had begun to weaken, and he could no longer parry reporters' questions or present himself the way he wanted to. He cut off interviews for good.

Considering *Ravelstein* a betrayal ignores Saul's basic approach to politics. Though he had supported many conservative social and cultural positions, Saul was never a true believer in the left or right. His sympathy with any position never extended to loyalty to an entire belief system, as even a cursory reading of his novels or the Atlas biography reveals. Soon after *Ravelstein*'s publication, we had a conversation about the inconsistency between espousing individual liberty and trying to control what happens in the bedroom, which pleasantly reminded me of times long ago when he and I puzzled together over the ironic and contradictory behavior of human beings.

A few years earlier, when James Atlas had approached Saul about becoming his biographer, my father agreed to cooperate. Atlas had written a biography of Delmore Schwartz and Saul liked it. After several conversations, no doubt thinking he could control Atlas, Saul granted him access to the archive at the University of Chicago's Regenstein Library, where, for decades and with his usual absence of forethought, he had deposited boxes full of highly revealing documents. The biographer took his task seriously, and Saul became alarmed when friends and relatives began to complain about his pointed questions. It became clear that Mr. Atlas was going to put in details Saul did not want included, and they quarreled. By then my father could not withdraw the consent that ceded full control. All Saul could do was feign a lack of interest when the biography was published.

I refused to speak with Atlas about my father, but I wanted to protect my deceased mother from a dismissive portrait like that in the literary memoir that Ruth Miller, Saul's former student, had published in 1991. I wrote a summary of her life for Atlas, and was pleased by the respect he showed for Anita. But the publication of *Bellow* in 2000 caused a stir in the family and among friends who complained that their statements were taken out of context and placed in too negative a light. My father, angered and hurt, sought someone to blame, and made the biography into yet another measure of family loyalty. In his acknowledgments Atlas overstated a friendship with Adam and Dan but made no mention of me. I became a momentary hero with Saul for limiting my participation to a simple sketch of his first wife.

Bellow affected me in ways I had not anticipated. As I read about events in a life I knew well, I began to seriously reconsider my public silence. Atlas's apparent idealization of my father as a great writer likely prompted him to become Saul's biographer. But speaking with detractors, ex-friends, and the few members of our family willing to cooperate seemed to have infected his once high opinion of my father with anger and disappointment that had crept into his biography. I began to wonder if my negative feelings about "old Saul" might infect the memoir I was considering.

I do not believe Saul understood that he was losing his short-term memory, but he knew something was wrong as he complained to my cousin Lesha about his *kopf*, Yiddish for head. My father also revealed a concern for his mental state in a 2000 letter to Philip Roth where, likely referring to the repetitions and gaps in his letters about the origins of his early novels, he thanked Roth for covering up for what he termed a breakdown.

By 2002 Saul's mental deterioration, which was akin to islands of clarity in a dark sea of silence, was beginning to accelerate. I decided it was time for one more real conversation that

I feared might be our last. Irritated for decades that Saul took only a passing interest in my adult life, I decided to tell my father something about who I was in a way he'd understand. When asked about writing, he often employed a quote from Stendhal about developing literary characters by giving them what they lack—that is, creating them out of essential bits and pieces. I decided the best way to describe myself was to adopt a parallel explanation and said, "I took from my family what I needed."

I began with Beebee's observation that I created a family for myself everywhere I went by remaining loyal to people I cared about. I elaborated that with a kaleidoscopic childhood like mine, I had fashioned my identity out of the bits and pieces I found in my family. I ended with a tribute to how Saul's warmth and vulnerability was central to my ability to love, to be a good person and father, and was the glue that kept the pieces of my personality in place.

When I finished, Saul praised me and the identity I had forged. But he touched me most deeply by referring to the times I called him in despair over the deaths of those I loved—Anita, Beebee, and George Sarant. "When you call me in that state," he said, "I can see the goodness in your soul." Who could ask more of an aging father? Had those been his last words to me, we would have been spared the greatest pain that ever came between us.

When my daughter Juliet and Charlie Schulman announced their engagement and set a wedding date in New York, Saul was genuinely excited. He continually referred to the date as if trying to make sure it was fixed in his mind. I took his insistence on "moving heaven and earth to get there" as a reflection of his desire to attend. Arrangements seemed to be on track, when Saul called Juliet a few weeks before the wedding. Offering no explanation, he said, "You must forgive me, but I cannot come to your wedding." Juliet and I had a heart-wrenching conversation about how Saul could inflict so much pain by making commitments and failing to fulfill them. For the first time, Juliet understood why I had erected the self-protective barriers between my father and myself that she had often observed and pointed out to me.

Saul did not call me until Adam warned him that not speaking directly to me would make matters worse. Saul called and simply announced he would not be at the wedding, again offering no explanation. I told Saul he was hurting me and my child, that this was unforgivable from a father and grandfather. When he pleaded innocence, I said, "Damn your soul," which was about the worst thing I could say to a man I knew to be preoccupied with its long-term fate.

A few days later Saul called back and laid the responsibility on his doctor, who forbade travel. But in his belated medical excuse, I recognized a familiar pattern of hiding behind someone else when he had done something hurtful. Adam tried to intercede, but by then Saul had his back up and refused to discuss it. Both brothers offered to go to Boston to help Saul, Janis, and Rosie come to New York. Adam even called Will, Saul's assistant, asking if there was any constructive way for him to intervene. Will said no, confirming my impression that Saul had dug in his heels and would not budge.

Saul's absence cast a shadow over an otherwise joyous day

for Juliet. But when there was not even a phone call to the bride and groom wishing them well, I knew that Saul was angry at being challenged by all three sons. Three weeks later, Saul traveled to Cincinnati, assisted by Dan, to see his sister Jane, and at Christmas he went to Toronto with Janis and Rosie. Clearly he was able to travel. I concluded he did not attend because, surrounded by those who knew him well, he could not hide memory losses and did not want to be embarrassed in public. Tragically, he had begun to ask after his brothers, only to be pained by the news of their deaths once again. Several times Saul decided to call his old friend Sam Freifeld, whose ex-wife had to repeat the news that Sam had passed away. My father grieved anew and complained that he hadn't been informed that his old friend had died, when of course he had.

But Saul did not level with me, or with Juliet, about why he did not attend, though it is likely that he was unable to face his own deterioration. After the wedding. I did not speak with Saul for eighteen months. I did not wish to see him, talk to him, or hear about him. My anger was so great and my suspicions were so high after he went to Cincinnati that I occasionally wondered if not coming to my daughter's wedding was his way of getting even for my absence from celebratory events in his honor. After some months, Saul asked Adam why he had not heard from me. My brother answered that it was because he had not attended Juliet's wedding. Saul began to repeat his medical rationale, but Adam said that he was just answering his question and did not want to discuss Saul's reasons.

Two letters I wrote during that 2003 rupture that were never answered convey the depth of my anger and despair, but they also reveal my awareness of the chronic sad state of affairs between us that had existed for decades.

(January 2003)

Dear Pop,

Your inability to move beyond your own needs, no matter what the obstacles to attending Juliet's wedding, has rent the fragile fabric that holds this family together.

The damage is to my family feeling and thus takes the form of my loss of interest in your welfare and in softening the burdens of your old age. I find within myself no desire for contact—to visit, to speak to you, or to hear family reports.

I cannot alter that perception or undo the damage it has caused. If this is something you wish to alter, the initiative rests with you.

If I do not hear from you, and I mean you—not surrogates—it means to me that either you did not receive this letter, you are incapable of remedying the situation, or the absence of a relationship going into the future is your desire.

In any case I remain your son—even in absentia.

G.

(May 2003)

Dear Pop,

I thought I'd write as I did not want a repeat of our last phone conversation [which occurred when he said he was not attending]. Unfortunately, this puts me in a position of continually circumscribing our relationship. There is not much left to talk about when you don't agree about politics, money, educational philosophy, or the nature of family obligations.

This is not my choice and it is not my desire. However, as we both get older changes have occurred. You have become less tolerant of differences between yourself and others. I have come to have faith in myself and the correctness of my own ideas.

I do not believe either of us will change because neither of us really wishes to abandon what we experience as positions which are correct for ourselves. I do not think it wise that we do. I do not believe that our relationship could withstand a truly candid discussion of our views. I wish this were not so but in my heart I believe it to be so.

Frankly I do not see a lot of positive options. But a relationship built on false confession would be worse than what we have. So here we are. As a child you are my pop and I love you. This will never change. As a man I will not abandon myself and you should not ask me to do so. I never mean to hurt you, but when it comes to a choice between my values and hurting someone—even you—my values will prevail. This is the man my parents brought me up to be and this is the man I am.

G.

Saul may have wanted to mend fences, but he was unable to bring himself to apologize to me or to his granddaughter. Instead he reverted to custom by enlisting a messenger. Though I had not been in touch with Monroe Engel, Saul's former editor at the Viking Press, for fifty years, I received an e-mail from him, gently trying to encourage me to visit my ailing father. As he showed no interest in my side of the story, I took him to be just another messenger on an errand from Saul.

About eighteen months later, there was a large party in Boston given by my wife JoAnn's sister. I called Will about visiting Saul. Though I particularly disliked talking to Saul on the phone when there was unresolved business between us, but the good-hearted Will insisted on putting him on the line. I told my father I'd be in Boston in a few weeks and would like to talk to him in person.

Saul had suffered a stroke, was bedridden, and was not expected to survive. When I arrived, Janis and Rosie were out. An attendant led me up to his room, where he drifted in and out of a sleeplike state. Saul recognized me and spoke coherently though softly. The family cat was also dozing on the bed, prompting me to call my father's present state a feline existence. "Exactly," he said, and a spark of life shone through as he quipped that it "made him want to scratch."

I needed to clear the air as we always had, particularly if this was to be our last conversation. With great trepidation, I said he had hurt me deeply by not attending Juliet's wedding. He answered, "I did not mean to hurt you, but the disease takes over." "But you did hurt me and my child!" I exclaimed. Just then his attendant came in, ostensibly to check on him, though she immediately insisted that Saul was a very sick man who could not tolerate any emotional upset. Alone again, I asked if there was anything more he wanted to say. He said no. I ended with "We always had an honest relationship, and I don't see any reason to change it now." He nodded in agreement. As I left to have lunch, the attendant was giving Janis, who had returned, a report. I concluded that she had been instructed to

listen at the door and interrupt if I brought up the problems between us.

I returned an hour later with a different concern, that I'd never see Saul alive again. I tried to find a way to say goodbye without using the word *death*. I was standing at his bedside and Saul put his hand on my heart. I told him that I loved him as I always had. I kissed him and walked out of his room. Saying "Goodbye, Pop" under my breath, I wished him a peaceful end.

Saul's statement that he wished me no harm went a long way toward healing my wound. For fifty years I had been protected from the kind of pain Saul could cause when he let people down: as a child by his love, and as an adult by physical distance and layers of emotional insulation. This time I had let my guard down out of my love for Juliet, and I had paid the price. Looking back, I realize that I had successfully avoided the full force of his coldness. The disappointment I had experienced was just a full dose of the selfishness everyone else had been enduring for years.

Although his memory had been failing for several years, Saul had insisted on teaching a course on Joseph Conrad at Boston University, but his problems were severe enough that Jame Wood was enlisted to coteach. Will, who attended, told m that my father could still make magnificent observations abo fiction, but could no longer follow the thread of the disci sions. During my final visits to him in Boston, Saul remin me of Beebee. Both walked aimlessly around homes that peared both familiar and unfamiliar. But I did not realize bad Saul's memory was until he forgot about a dinner gue invited after clearing it with him and Janis the day b When the young man arrived, Saul raked me over the

for inviting a stranger into the house. He backed off after a head shake from Janis, which indicated he was relying on her when his memory failed.

The extent of Janis's control over his literary affairs became clear after I mentioned a growing desire to gain access to Saul's archive in the Regenstein Library. "So," Saul said with pleasure, "you're getting interested in your past." His signature was necessary for me to gain access, and Will began to make the necessary arrangements. After an unduly long delay, Will called to tell me that my access to the archive had been denied. Diplomatically, he added that matters were out of his hands and in those of the Wylie Agency. Though I made it clear to Saul's new literary agent that Saul approved of my request, I received a curt refusal from the same young man who had sweetly quoted romantic poetry to Saul in Vermont. By then I saw that my father did not even have the power to give me access to his own archive.

The final blow was determining Saul's final resting place. By the late 1980s, my aunt Jane and Saul were the only survivors from the generation of Bellows that had lived in Lachine. Though Morrie was buried in Georgia and Sam in Israel, Saul retained a deep faith that he'd see members of his family after his death. For a decade that faith took on a very concrete form: a preoccupation with being buried next to his parents. But Jane's husband, Charlie, and their sons Larry and Bob were in a plot next to my grandparents. The one remaining spot was reserved for her. Saul was irritated that his sister, once again, took precedence, but a solution became available.

An adjacent gravesite, sufficient to hold Saul, Lesha, and her husband, was for sale. Lesha made the initial arrangements but

needed her uncle's go-ahead. Burial next to his parents would confirm the sentimental connection between Saul and his family of origin in perpetuity. But when Lesha pressed Saul for a decision, she was met with obfuscation and delay. Finally, with my father present but silent, it was Janis who told Lesha that the two of them would be buried together in Vermont. With one sentence, Janis finally eliminated any possibility of interference by Saul's family during the rest of his life and even in death.

During his final year, Saul was very weak and rarely left his bed. Every time I asked about his welfare on the phone, his answer, "Hunky-dory," made me realize my father was too far gone to realize how frail he was. I tracked Saul's health through Will's phone reports. Eventually, it turned so dire that I took a red-eye from San Francisco to Boston, arriving at 6:00 A.M. The winter temperature was 2 degrees. I snoozed at the airport until the temperature went up to 4 and got a chuckle out of Saul when I reported that a 100 percent improvement was sufficient for me to leave the comfort of the terminal.

Apparently it had been a long time since Saul had ventured downstairs, but that day he pulled himself together and met me on the first floor. Janis, who was in and out of the house all day, was delighted to see him dressed and sitting upright. Maria, the kind woman now charged with his physical care, reported that Saul called me his "little boy" and spoke of me often. My father's mental state had indeed worsened. The seas of silence had expanded and the islands of clarity were smaller. He often became lost midthought but seemed to understand when I brought him up to speed about my family, and even inquired whether I was close to retirement.

My hair had been as white as Saul's for decades, and on that visit I sported a large beard, also white. As the afternoon drew to a close and my departure grew near, Saul said he was glad to see "sonny boy." By mimicking Al Jolson's intonation, Saul was bringing to mind the times I sat on his lap as a boy and he made believe my stomach was a cello, drawing his arm back and forth as he sang, "Climb upon my knee, sonny boy."

"Yes, Pop," I answered, "even under all this snow [Bellowese for my white hair and beard], I'll always be your sonny boy." After decades of being nearly buried, "young Saul" and little Herschele reemerged in our last moment together. I left as Janis prepared a beautiful Sabbath table to celebrate Saul's coming downstairs on a Friday night. I believe it was the last time he did so under his own power.

Saul and I had a few brief telephone calls in the ensuing weeks. I remember shouting into the phone, "I love you, sweetheart," the last thing I ever said to my father.

Chapter Eleven

EXPANDING THE FRANCHISE

WILL WARNED ME that Saul was failing. His breathing was so labored that trying to speak to him on the phone was useless. I spent the day he died on tenterhooks, anticipating the call from Boston that never came. My father's lawyer, Walter Pozen, called the media and word of Saul Bellow's death was circulated almost immediately. Juliet heard of her grandfather's death via the media. My noble daughter tried to spare me from the coldness she had already suffered, frantically calling every place I might be, without success. I sat in stunned silence after turning on my car radio and hearing the news.

I was already angered by Walter's apparent lack of concern. A few days after Saul died my brother Dan wryly noted that even after a horrific traffic accident, the state police show more decency toward the family than Walter showed Saul's children. He went out of his way to make a statement that Saul's mental state was "sharp to end," which was completely at variance with my observations of my father's decline. Since Walter's public version of events was so different from the shrinking islands of lucidity in the expanding sea of dark silences, along with Saul's frequent memory lapses and confusion, I eventually considered Walter's gratuitous assertion of mental clarity to be a preemptive attempt to mythologize Saul Bellow, the famous author, at the expense of my father, the man.

As Jewish tradition requires burial before the Sabbath, JoAnn and I flew across the country overnight. The stark simplicity of Orthodox ritual we followed in Brattleboro's Jewish cemetery made Saul's death all too palpable. Pins with black ribbons were affixed to the mourners and were roughly torn to represent our loss and grief. Saul's thin wooden casket was so light I had to remind myself that we were carrying my father, who had often seemed larger-than-life. At the gravesite, the black cloth with a white Star of David was removed from the casket and Saul was lowered into the ground. Next to the rectangular hole stood a pile of sand with a shovel placed back side up to represent the unusual task to which it was about to be put. Janis carefully balanced a bit of sand on the shovel's back and threw it onto the casket, where it landed with a hollow sound. Next came my turn. I picked up a handful of sand, kissed it, said, "Rest easy, Pop," and threw it into the hole. Adam and Dan followed with their shovels of sand before the other mourners took their turns at the required task of filling the grave level to the earth.

When our cousin Shael took a turn, I blurted out, "Put one in for Grandpa," and so he did. He labeled several more: one for Jane, one for his father Sam, and two for Morrie, whom we all agreed required an extra because he took a double share of everything. I took another turn and labeled one shovelful for each first cousin—Larry, Bobby, and Lynn—who were all deceased. After the grave was filled, the rabbi outlined a six-foot rectangle above the casket. Janis placed a temporary metal marker on the grave and lovingly smoothed the sand around it. The rabbi led all assembled in the Jewish prayer for the dead. The family walked away between two rows of mourners.

About a hundred family members and friends assembled in a nearby building, ate and drank a bit, and listened to short speeches, one by Ruth Wisse about Saul's Jewishness and another by Martin Amis about his literary legacy. The rabbi ended with a tribute to the unique love between Janis and Saul that solidified my view of how she romanticized their relationship.

My family joined Lesha's at Dan and Heather's home, where we shared family stories over dinner. A few days later, JoAnn and I took the train to New York City, passing the old house in Tivoli. We went to the newly remodeled MoMA, where looking at the pictures was like visiting old friends I had shared with Saul on dozens of custodial visits. As we passed through galleries, I found myself humming an aria from Mozart's *Marriage of Figaro*, which had filled our house every morning as he finished *Augie March*.

Back in California, I felt a minimum of sadness at Saul's passing. Alexandra's comment, that he had lived life to the fullest, pretty much summed up my feelings. The grief I experienced was balanced by my family's love and the kind wishes of innumerable friends.

Three memorials emphasizing Saul Bellow, the famous author, were orchestrated by his literary agent. They began to reshape my views about my father and his legacy. The New York and Boston memorials included no family members and took little note of the father or the man. Being considered irrelevant to memorials celebrating our father angered all of

Saul's sons. I ardently wished to speak at the service in his honor at the University of Chicago, the school that had profoundly influenced him but also shaped the intellectual life of my mother, me, my wife, along with dozens of family members and friends.

My request to Janis was placed in the hands of the Wylie Agency. Somehow five minutes were found. I spoke after Mayor Daley's amusing anecdotes about Saul lecturing at a campaign rally until the mayor had to remind my father that he, not Saul, was the candidate. I carefully chose my words, expressing a collective family debt to the university and emphasizing how Saul embodied its pervasive questioning spirit.

I was followed by Jeffrey Eugenides, whose uneasy tribute to a man he had never met typified how I felt Saul's new literary agent had turned what should have been a moment of sorrow for those who knew and loved Saul as a human being into a marketing opportunity. I shared my father's concerns, and likely those of Janis, about the waning of Saul's literary star during his final decades. My father's lack of political correctness and bitter criticism of African American and women authors did little to endear him to critics, readers, or academia. Saul was pained by the infrequent use of his books in the classroom as novels with more nuanced considerations of race and gender gained popularity on college campuses.

Making the memorial services into publicity events filled with literary lights who didn't even know my father brought to my mind Andrew Wylie's boast (published in Harriet Wasserman's memoir) about turning a client "from a cash cow into a cash bull." I remember thinking that Saul Bellow, who was being promoted even in death, was now clearly in the grip of the

Philistines, people who emphasized money rather than culture, about whom he had complained for decades.

My personal communication with Janis had slowed before Saul died. Now letters came from lawyers, junior members of Walter Pozen's firm, who were all very proper as they distributed the funds willed to Saul's children and grandchildren. In stages the extent of Janis's control in the shaping of my father's literary image became more and more clear. After a suitable interval, Janis asked Zachary Leader to be Saul's new biographer and enlisted Benjamin Taylor to collect and publish his letters, which show Saul's magnificent way of expressing himself and may well encourage new readers. Saul's archive was placed under the control of a committee headed by Janis, Walter Pozen, Martin Amis, and Philip Roth. At first, I despaired of gaining access to a portion of his literary side that was not published. Then I got mad and decided not to ask again.

Anita and Basil's house was filled with art, pottery, and books they had collected for decades, and now those objects populate my house and those of Basil's children. In his seventy years of the gypsy life, Saul had always traveled light. He had made no mention of personal items that might remind his sons of him. In anticipation, on my last visit I pinched one of the fedoras he so loved. Later, at my request, Janis sent one of the recorders Saul loved to play, canes for Lesha and me, bow ties for Andrew, baseball caps for Juliet, as well as a few more items I shared with my brothers and their children.

Saul did bequeath a few items. When my brothers went to Vermont to pick up a desk that Saul had left to Dan, Janis once again extolled the unique love she felt for our father. In an obviously prepared speech, Janis insisted, over and over, that there had been no problems between them, but her tone was so shrill that she demonstrated to my bewildered brothers the huge toll nursing Saul for a decade had actually taken.

During the quiet lull that mercifully followed the hubbub right after Saul's death, I decided to reread all of my father's published works. Slowly, what began as a reaction to a grave robbery became an opportunity to appreciate his public side and even to reconsider my lifelong protective behavior toward him, as well as my silence. To better understand why I had so fiercely protected Saul, I had to turn the question about family loyalty I had for Philip Roth after reading *Patrimony*—has Philip no shame?—back onto myself.

Saul's life was filled with misunderstandings and conflicts. For years I observed that despite his denials, personal and literary criticisms stung my father, prompting running battles with family, former friends, reviewers, and critics. With few exceptions, he thought these battles stemmed from the inability of others to understand the artist in him, not from his own sensitivity. He took umbrage at disagreements small and large. For decades, I volunteered to protect the author, but I had actually been shielding the private man I knew to be so easily hurt. In telling him and myself that I was protecting our private relationship, I was subscribing to my father's taboo about crossing a line between work and art that he had created and then proceeded to cross from the first pages of *Dangling Man* to the end of *Ravelstein*.

My insistence on protecting Saul Bellow the author was to change only after I spoke in depth with Janna Malamud two years after my father's death. Janna's early life mirrored mine. She had been raised in a household devoted to writing, and her father, Bernard Malamud, had promulgated artistic values similar to Saul's. Janna had written two books about her father. The first defended the artist's privacy, while the second, written years later, was a revealing literary memoir of growing up with a writer father.

After reading both, I contacted Janna to ask why she had changed her mind. Her candor about protecting herself as she protected her father helped me realize that my public silence extended beyond shielding Saul's creativity as he wrote. The public/private line I had refused to cross combined *two* of Saul's views: one on protecting the art, and another on protecting the artist. But Janna's father and mine had conflated the precarious state of art in creation that literally took place behind a closed door with the absolute need to protect them just because they were *artists*, period. Janna confessed to blindly buying into the merger, and so, I realized, had I.

Andrew's wedding, about a year later, gave me an opportunity to have a meeting of the minds with Adam and Dan. We all resented being shunted aside, barred from access to Saul's archive, and rued the costs of continued silence. Each brother wished to come to terms with being Saul's son. As it turned out, my lack of access to his archive proved to be a blessing in disguise. With my conversation with Janna fresh in my mind, I found a truer inheritance in my memories of Saul as a father, as a man, and in the traces of himself in his novels and essays. Humanizing the complexity of all three aspects of Saul Bellow in this memoir is my contribution to a franchise my father deserves.

Chapter Twelve

A GLANCE BACK AND
A GLANCE FORWARD

WRITER IS THE one-word descriptor on Saul Bellow's gravestone, a final testament to a life where everything and everyone was subordinated to art. After rereading his soul-searching novels, this time as a memoirist, I find a man trying to understand his inability to live in harmony with others and with himself. Saul simply never fit in, and every corner of his life was strewn with evidence of an inability to just get along. Musing about his character with his longtime friend Gene Goodheart shortly before his death, Saul remained plagued by doubts, asking aloud, "Was I a man or a jerk?"

My easily wounded father received partial protection from his opacity, his rational explanations, his disinclination to introspect, and the firm mental line he maintained between his art and his life. Writing a memoir enabled me to see that by making himself the only one able to cross that line in the privacy of his study was what allowed Saul to plumb his feelings, place them into his narrators, and imbue his fiction with the power to deeply touch his readers. Saul Bellow could not do so without tapping into the emotions that were inseparable from the life he most cared about: his own.

In the end I do not know how well Saul understood himself. But his frequent and vehement protests about being misunderstood and about the inaccessibility of the inner life shed an essential light. It was and remains my distinct impression that he believed the real action occurs inside human beings. I am sure his cultivation of *my* looking inward during the decades of our "real conversations" was to impart that all-important message to his son.

But looking back at how he used the term *inner life* over a lifetime, even "young Saul" did not identify the content of his. His "inner life," like the human imagination, was infinite but private. What little my father said directly about feelings needs to be supplemented by observing how he acted and considering what he wrote. When "old Saul" added a more spiritual meaning that encompassed a soul that might outlive the human body, the "inner life" became even less accessible to Saul and, in his eyes, to mankind. In his essays, in his books, and in person he complained that modern man had lost his inner moral compass and the guidance it provides. But alienation from the "inner life" represented a danger for Saul in this life and an even greater one as he contemplated how to move into the next.

I have come to believe Saul feared that he had harmed or even deadened not only his heart but even his soul by erecting so many self-protective barriers. What if the precious vessel, the soul that was to carry him into the next life, proved inaccessible because the gap between his rational side and his inner life was too great to traverse? Saul's incessant late-life refrain about the inaccessibility of mankind's deepest human feelings reflects a recognition that he, too, was afflicted with the condition he so accurately diagnosed in society but could not alter there or in himself. And worse, that the damage may have been self-inflicted.

Saul's soul may or may not live on, but, judging by the public reactions to the recent publication of his letters, the conflation of the man and his work persists outside of the Bellow family. Reviewers, swept away by reexposure to his lofty prose, seemed unwilling to ask the obvious final question that Saul posed about his character: How could the same man so inspire in a literary letter and be so prickly, bilious, and self-justifying in a personal one?

The answer lies in the ambiguities that were Saul Bellow, which spawned so many narratives tinged with filial overtones. He was, after all, a man who lived for a singular creative purpose; a man who struggled with his deepest emotions; an author touched with literary genius; an author who became duly famous; an authority with wisdom to impart; a father recently passed away; a father largely absent but emotionally present; and a man, father, and husband who promised more than he could deliver. And I was his little boy: a boy who felt deeply cared about; a grown son deeply influenced by the kind of love he received; and a man wrestling with the challenges of relating to a difficult father who walked away from shared family ideals.

The public aspects of my father have infused the image of Saul Bellow, the famous author, with the same universal magnetic power to live on that is afforded to heroes, to symbols, and to the literary characters that he created. But emphasizing the literary lion overlooks the very human man and masks the essential soft side of Saul I find in his final published letter, wherein a dreamy old man returns to the paradise he made of Lachine. He recalls standing at his mother's side as they looked longingly at a pair of patent leather shoes Saul called "elegantissimo" in a store window. Somehow Lescha procured them, and Saul honored her use of scarce family assets by polishing them with butter. An already touching story of maternal indulgence takes on added meaning when compared to Sam's request to his father for a suit to commemorate his bar mitzvah, which resulted in a beating.

Parents, tender or harsh, die. Heroes and symbols do not. When readers continue to imbue his characters and their creator with personal meaning, they bring to Saul Bellow a form of immortality—though one vastly different from the spiritual forms he worked and hoped for. It is, nonetheless, a form I believe he would have found most pleasing.

Even though a heroic status masks crucial aspects of the man, I have resigned myself to sharing my father with his literary public because I have no real choice. As a man whose respect for symbols to carry deep meaning equals that of my father, I must graciously bow to his status as a literary hero that will continue to influence public perceptions of Saul Bellow, the famous author.

Writing a memoir has made Saul a more nuanced man to his firstborn: a father, a duly famous writer, and a symbol of literary heroism. Writing a memoir was not, as I anticipated, about staying close to "young Saul." By adopting his daily writing habits, I found a delightful new connection with the parts of my father that I once found alien and intimidating, which have now brought me closer to the "old Saul" on whom I turned my back. And doubtless the loss of privacy, his and mine, that will follow publication of my memoir will bring more—I hope positive—surprises.

APPENDIX OF NOVELS AND NARRATORS

BRIEF SUMMARY DISCUSSIONS OF ALL SAUL BELLOW'S
WORKS ARE AVAILABLE ONLINE AT THE *SAUL BELLOW
JOURNAL*, WWW.SAULBELLOW.ORG

Publication	Narrator
Dangling Man (1944)	Joseph
The Victim (1947)	Asa Leventhal
The Adventures of Augie March (1953)	Augie March
Seize the Day (1956)	Tommy Wilhelm
Henderson the Rain King (1959)	Eugene Henderson
Herzog (1964)	Moses Herzog
The Last Analysis: A Play (1965)	
Mr. Sammler's Planet (1969)	Artur Sammler
Humboldt's Gift (1975)	Charlie Citrine
To Jerusalem and Back (1976)	
The Dean's December (1982)	Albert Corde
Him with His Foot in His Mouth (1984)	

More Die of Heartbreak (1987)	Kenneth Trachtenberg
A Theft (1989)	Ithiel Regler
It All Adds Up: Essays (1994)	
The Actual (1997)	Harry Trellman
Ravelstein (2000)	Chick
Collected Stories (2001)	

ACKNOWLEDGMENTS

I have long struggled to capture subtle personal meanings in a written form that will touch readers who are strangers to me and to my father.

Three people who knew both of us proved invaluable as the work progressed. To my wife, who found love on every page of a shaky first draft I could show no one else, I owe a debt that cannot be measured. Mitzi McClosky and Gene Goodheart, longtime friends of Saul's and of mine, generously agreed to be my first outside readers. I took heart from Mitzi's praise for a book I knew Saul would have hated and wisdom from Gene telling me I could and should do better.

While it was difficult to hear criticism, in almost every instance I moved to address the shortcomings pointed out by Robert Cornfield, Ramsay Breslin, Elise Miller, Elizabeth Stein, and the members of the San Francisco Bay Area Psychobiography Study Group, who correctly found fault in draft after draft while urging me forward.

As those years of writing in solitude came to an end, Kimberly Witherspoon of Inkwell Management, ably assisted by

William Callahan, saw an elegant little book therein and Nancy Miller of Bloomsbury found a memoir that, with her help and that of Lea Beresford as well, I am pleased to have completed.

A thank-you for waiting is due to many who checked their curiosity and were patient until a very picky author was satisfied. They are my children, Juliet and Andrew; my brothers, Adam and Dan; my stepmothers Sasha and Alexandra; my cousin Lesha; Miriam Tarcov; and friends and relatives with whom I have spoken during the five years I have been working on a book that I hope will touch them as well.

A NOTE ON THE AUTHOR

GREGORY BELLOW, PH.D., was a psychoanalytically ori-
ented psychotherapist for forty years and remains a member of
the core faculty of the Sanville Institute for Clinical Social Work.
He lives in Redwood City, California.